REVISE KEY STAGE 2 SATs
Mathematics

REVISION WORKBOOK

Expected Standard

Series Consultant: Janice Pimm

Authors: Giles Clare and Paul Flack

This revision workbook is written for students who aim to perform at the expected national standard in Mathematics in their Year 6 SATs.

For students who hope to perform above the expected standard, check out:

Revise Key Stage 2 SATs Mathematics Revision Guide:
Above Expected Standard 9781292146256

Revise Key Stage 2 SATs Mathematics Revision Workbook:
Above Expected Standard 9781292146270

For the full range of Pearson revision titles visit:
www.pearsonschools.co.uk/revise

ALWAYS LEARNING

PEARSON

Contents

Number

Calculation

Fractions, decimals and percentages

Ratio and proportion

Algebra

Measurement

Geometry

Statistics

A small bit of small print

The Standards and Testing Agency publishes Sample Test Materials on its website. This is the official content and this book should be used in conjunction with it. The questions in this book have been written to help you practise what you have learned in your revision. Remember: the real test questions may not look like this.

Introduction

About your tests

At the end of Year 6, you will take tests to find out about your maths skills. This book will help you revise all of the important skills you need for your tests.

- There will be one **arithmetic** test. This test will ask you to carry out calculations. You will have 30 minutes to do this test.

- There will be two **reasoning** tests. These tests will ask you to solve problems. You will have 40 minutes to do each test.

Using this book

Each page of this book is about a different maths skill. Use the checkboxes at the top of the page to track your progress:

Had a look   ☑   Tick this box when you've read the page.

Nearly there   ☑   Tick this box when you understand the page quite well.

Nailed it!   ☑   Tick this box when you understand the page really well.

+marks 11/11

Place value

1. Label each digit in the number below. One has been done for you.

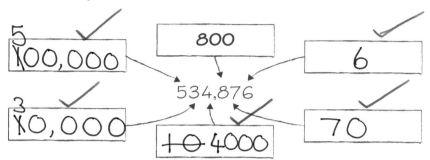

5
100,000 ✓

3
10,000 ✓

800 ✓

534,876

+0 4000 ✓

6 ✓

70 ✓

> Make sure you write the correct number of zeros.

5 marks 5

2. Write these numbers in figures.

a) Two thousand, six hundred and forty-three

2643 ✓

> Read the whole number before writing it down.

b) Nine hundred and seventy-five thousand, six hundred and forty-eight

975,648 ✓

c) Six million, six hundred and fourteen thousand, two hundred and fifteen

6,614,215 ✓

3 marks 3

3. Write these numbers in words.

a) 7,390   Seven thousand, x 3 three hun-dred and ninty. ✓

> Say the number out loud before writing the words.

b) 18,326   Eighteen thousand three hund-red and twenty six. ✓

c) 455,201   Four hundred and fifty five, two hundred and one. ✓

3 marks 3

1

Negative numbers

1. Find the difference between the temperatures.
   One has been done for you.

   > Use a number line. The difference is the size of the gap between the numbers.

   a) 7 °C and −2 °C   ....9 degrees...........

   b) −8 °C and −4 °C   ....

   c) 14 °C and −22 °C ....

   d) −8 °C and 22 °C   ....

   4 marks

2. Write the missing numbers in the boxes.

   a)

   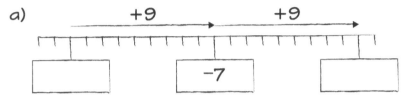

   b)

   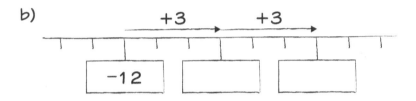

   c)

   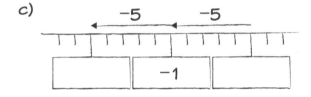

   6 marks

3. Alex is on the London Underground. The train has stopped at Bank Station, which is 41.4 m below the ground. Magda is on the second floor of a building, which is 6.7 m above the ground. How much higher up is Magda than Alex?

   ....

   .... **1 mark**

4. The temperature in Stockholm on Monday was 3 °C. The temperature fell by 4 degrees on Tuesday and then rose by 7 degrees on Wednesday. What was the temperature on Wednesday?

   ....

   .... **2 marks**

Decimal numbers

1. Write the numbers in figures.

   a) Six point seven   ....

   b) Nine point four three   ....

   c) Eighteen point five two eight ....

   d) Six point zero four three   ....   **4 marks**

2. Draw arrows to show where the numbers go on the number line.

   | 2.21 | | 2.81 | | 3.14 |

   2   2.5   3   3.5   4

   | 2.15 | | 3.43 | | 3.75 |

   6 marks

3. Use the signs < and > to show which is greater.

   a) 4.6 > 4.06   b) 9.7 ☐ 9.89

   c) 6.56 ☐ 5.98   d) 23.5 ☐ 2.35

   e) 2.22 ☐ 2.222   f) 1.001 ☐ 0.101   **6 marks**

4. Anil finished a race in 14.7 seconds, Lucy finished in 13.2 seconds and
   Max finished in 13.7 seconds. Who finished first, second and third?

   first   ....
   second   ....
   third   ....   **1 mark**

5. Use the number cards to make three numbers that are greater than
   7 and have 3 decimal places.

   | 4 | | 5 | | 6 | | 7 |

   ....

   3 marks

Rounding

1. Round to the nearest 100

   a) 5,325   ....**5,300**....

   b) 8,431   ..**8400**.. ✓

   c) 13,678 ..**14,600**.. ✗ 13,700

                             ~~2~~ 1   3 marks

2. Round to the nearest 1,000

   a) 4,376   ..**4000**.. ✓

   b) 18,501   ..**19,500**.. ✗ 19,000

   c) 547,679 ..**548,000**.. ✓

                             2   3 marks

3. Draw lines to match the numbers to the rounded values.

   a) 4,638,420 to the nearest 10,000   5,249,000 ✗

   b) 4,637,300 to the nearest 1,000,000   5,000,000 ✗

   c) 5,248,612 to the nearest 1,000   4,640,000 ✓

   d) 5,220,230 to the nearest 100,000   5,200,000 ✗   1   4 marks

4. Round the numbers to the right values. Some of question a) has been done for you.

   a) 7,452,540

      To the nearest 1,000,000   ..**7,000,000**..

      To the nearest 100,000   ..**7,500,000**..

      To the nearest 10,000   ..**7,460,000** ✗ 745,0000..

      To the nearest 1,000   ..**7,452,000** ✗..

   b) 4,250,500

      To the nearest 1,000,000   ..**4,000,000**..

      To the nearest 100,000   ..**4,300,000**..

      To the nearest 10,000   ..**4,250,000**..

      To the nearest 1,000   ..**4,251,000**..

                                  6 marks

Rounding decimals

1. Round these numbers to 1 decimal place.

a) 6.42 ...6.4... ✓

b) 4.68 ...4.7...

c) 13.85 ...13.9...

d) 2.057 ...2.1...

> To round to 1 decimal place, look at the hundredths. To round to 2 decimal places, look at the thousandths.

4 marks

2. Round these numbers to 2 decimal places.

a) 8.662 ...8.66.

b) 7.554 ...75.56

c) 75.555 ...7.55...

d) 27.0808 ...7....

4 marks

3. Circle all the numbers that round to 4.5 to 1 decimal place.

(4.53)   4.55   (5.45)   (4.48)   4.41   (4.45)

1 mark

4. Use the number cards to make the 2-place decimal number that is closest to 7. You can only use each card once.

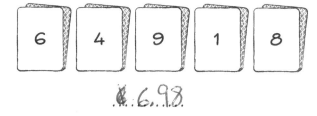

| 6 | 4 | 9 | 1 | 8 |

...6.98...

1 mark

5. Emma used a calculator to work out the following calculations. Round each answer to 2 decimal places.

a) 16.351 × 7 = 114.457   ...114.46....

b) 22 ÷ 7 = 3.1428571429   ...3.14......

c) 50 ÷ 6 = 8.3333333333   ...8.33......

d) 70 ÷ 6 = 11.666666666666   ...11.67......

e) 27 ÷ 8 = 3.375   ....

5 marks

5

Roman numerals

1. Draw hands on the clock to show the right time.

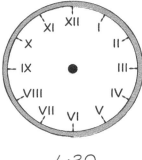   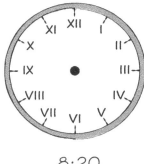   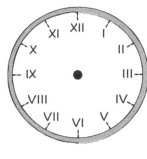

      4:30   8:20   9:35   3 marks

2. Write these Roman numerals in figures. One has been done for you.

   a) MMCCXV ....2,215............   b) MDL ....

   c) MCMXLV ....   d) MMXVI ....

                                                         3 marks

3. Complete these calculations. Give your answers in Roman numerals.

   a) X + VI = ...

   ....

   b) MCDL – CCXXVII = ...

   ....

                                                        2 marks

4. Yasmin looks at a sundial in the park. The shadow on the dial points to halfway between VI and VII. What time could it be?

   Sundials don't show minutes. The shadow is like the hour hand on a clock.

   ....

                                                      1 mark

5. Seth looks at an old clock. The small hand is between VII and VIII. The big hand is pointing at IV. What time is it?

   .... 1 mark

6. A DVD box says a movie was filmed in MCMLXXXIV. What year is this?

   .... 1 mark

Number and rounding problems

1. Find two different Roman numerals that add up to the number shown.
   One has been done for you.

   a) X = I + IX

   b) L = [＿＿＿] + [＿＿＿]

   c) M = [＿＿＿] + [＿＿＿]

   > I = 1, V = 5, X = 10,
   > L = 50, C = 100,
   > D = 500, M = 1,000

   2 marks

2. At an athletics event, a gold medal is given to the fastest runner, a silver medal is given to the second fastest and a bronze medal is given to the third fastest.

   <u>Race 1</u>

   Sanna 14._7 seconds　　Sam 14.59 seconds　　Chris 14.9 seconds

   <u>Race 2</u>

   Nellie 59._5 seconds　　Niraj 60.01 seconds　　Corinne 59.40 seconds

   a) Sanna's time rounded to 1 decimal place was 14.7 seconds. What was her time?

   .... seconds

   b) Nellie's time rounded to 1 decimal place was the same as Corinne's. What was her time?

   .... seconds

   c) Put the Race 2 times in order to show who won gold, silver and bronze. Write a name in each box.

   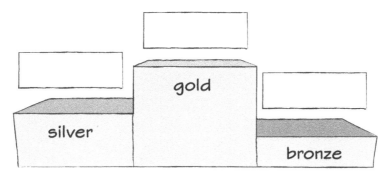

   5 marks

3. Will the answer be higher or lower than the first number in the calculation?
   Circle the correct answer.

   a) 43 − 27 = (higher / lower)　　　b) 6 + −5 = (higher / lower)

   c) −8 + 4 = (higher / lower)　　　d) −45 + −8 = (higher / lower)　**4 marks**

Written addition

1. Complete the calculations. One has been done for you.

   a) 4,272 + 5,676 =

   b) 5,879 + 2,964 =

```
    4 2 7 2
    5 6 7 6
  +   1
    9 9 4 8
```
        9,948   ....

   c) 16,743 + 2,528 =

   d) 9.68 + 542.09 =

              ....

                                                        3 marks

2. Asha has £216.50 in her bank account. She is given
   £75 birthday money, which she puts in the bank.
   How much money is in her bank account now?

   > Line up the digits carefully. Where do the decimal points go?

                        ....   **1 mark**

3. On Monday Bevan walked 3,276 steps and Reuben
   walked 2,860. On Tuesday Bevan walked 3,673 steps
   and Reuben walked 4,329. How many steps did each
   of them walk in total?

   > Read the question twice to make sure you understand.

              Bevan ....

              Reuben ....   **2 marks**

Written subtraction

1. Complete the calculations. One has been done for you.

a) 472 – 61 =

$$\begin{array}{r} 472 \\ -\ 61 \\ \hline 4\ 1\ 1 \end{array}$$

......411......

b) 579 – 264 =

....

> Move from the next column if you need to.

c) 836.4 – 524.2 =

....

d) 16,743 – 2,521 =

....

e) 753 – 64 =

....

f) 694.23 – 557.35 =

....

5 marks

2. Caleb buys a burger, fries and a cola. This is a total of 1,025 calories. He then swaps his cola (170 calories) for water (0 calories). How many calories does his meal have now?

.... 1 mark

3. Monika has £26.50 in her bank account. She spends £8.25 on a birthday present for her sister. How much money does she have left in her bank account?

> Make sure you keep any decimal points in line.

.... 1 mark

4. Sarah finished a Sports Day race in 14.45 seconds. Amina is 1.8 seconds faster than Sarah and Casey is 2.55 seconds faster than Amina. What were Amina and Casey's times?

Amina ....

Casey .... 2 marks

Estimating

1. Find approximate answers to these calculations.

   a) 5,239 + 7,320 + 897 = ...

   b) 0.83 + 0.45 + 0.21 = ...

   c) 1,548,629 + 3,492,587 = ...

   d) £10 − £3.67 = ...

   > Decide which place value to round to, depending on the question. Often the highest place value is best.

   4 marks

2. Connor and Mabel went shopping. Here are the prices from the shop.

Shoes.........	£45.99	Socks............	£4.99
Jacket........	£54.99	Hat...............	£12.99
Top	£21.99	Shorts...........	£8.99

   a) Connor bought a jacket, a hat and a pair of socks. Estimate how much he spent.

      £...............

   b) Mabel bought a hat, a jacket, two pairs of socks and a pair of shorts. Estimate how much she spent.

      £...............

   2 marks

3. A plane from London to New York takes 7 hours and 55 minutes. After 3 hours and 45 minutes, approximately how long is left?

   .... hours

   > The answer space will sometimes tell you what value to round to.

   1 mark

4. Roshan is building a rectangular fence around his garden. Two sides are each 12.6 m long and the other two sides are each 7.3 m long. Estimate how many metres he should buy.

   .... m

   1 mark

Add/subtract problems

1. A bus leaves the station with some passengers on board.

   At the first stop, they collect 6 more people.
   At the next stop, 11 people get off and 5 get on.
   When they reach the high street, 4 more people get off the bus. At the last stop, the remaining 8 passengers get off the bus.

   How many people were on the bus at the start of the journey?

   > Start with how many passengers were on the bus at the end of the journey and work backwards.

   ....   **2 marks**

2. Members of a cycling club are raising money for charity by cycling from Settle to Carlisle in three days.

   The route has a total distance of 88.2 miles. On the first day they cycle 37.7 miles to Kirkby Stephen. On the second day they cycle a further 26.1 miles to Penrith.

   How far do they need to cycle on the third day?

   > Work out the distance they have travelled so far and then subtract this from the total distance.

   ....   **2 marks**

3. Jahan and Niamh go shopping. They have £40 of birthday money each.

   Jahan buys clothes worth £4.99, £7.99 and £25.99. Niamh buys computer games worth £12.99, £16.99 and £7.99.

   What is the difference between the amount of change they each have?

   > Add the amounts by adjusting the prices to the nearest pound. Then, subtract the extra pennies.

   ....   **2 marks**

11

Multiples

1. Circle the multiples.

   a) Multiples of 4   76   24   18   90   8

   b) Multiples of 7   32   19   490   6   63

   c) Multiples of 9   180   27   99   18   72

   d) Multiples of 6   35   366   354   380   38   **4 marks**

2. Put these numbers into the right place in the table.

   14   15   26   29   32

   35   49   56

	multiple of 7	not a multiple of 7
even number		16
odd number	21	

   > Complete one column at a time. Write the even multiples of 7 and then the odd multiples of 7. Then write the even and odd numbers that are not multiples of 7

   2 marks

3. Write two common multiples of each set of numbers.

   a) 3 and 4   .... and ....

   b) 6 and 8   .... and ....

   c) 9 and 3   .... and ....

   d) 7 and 5   .... and ....   **4 marks**

4. Lily is setting out chairs in the school hall. She has 450 chairs and sets out 30 chairs in each row. How many rows of chairs will there be?

   ....

   ....   **1 mark**

5. Ellie says 1,345,360 is a multiple of 5 and a multiple of 2. Is she right? Explain how you know.

   ....

   ....   **1 mark**

Factors

1. List all the factors of each number.

   a) 42 ....

   b) 15 ....

   c) 72 ....

   d) 13 .... **4 marks**

2. Put these numbers into the right place in the table.

   21   8   6   42   4   1   12   19   7   14

   2   25   24   3   16   48

factors of 42	factors of 48

   Some of the numbers may not go in either column. Some may be common factors and go in both.

   4 marks

3. Amelia and Emily have 56 buns on a cake stall.
   They want to arrange them in rows.
   What possible arrangements could they use?

   ....

   .... **2 marks**

   Find pairs of factors so you don't miss any.

4. Look at this calculation.

   $6 \times 3 = 18$

   Are these statements true or false?

   a) 18 is a factor of 3   ....

   b) 3 is a factor of 18   ....

   c) 18 is a factor of 6   ....

5. Arthur says that 6 and 7 are both factors of 8,442. Is he right?
   How do you know?

   ....

   ....

Prime numbers

1. List all the prime numbers between these number pairs.

   a) 0 and 10 ....

   b) 10 and 20 ....

   c) 20 and 30 ....

   d) 30 and 40 .... **4 marks**

2. Are these statements true or false?
   How do you know?

   > Read each statement carefully. Think of an example to help explain your answer.

   a) All prime numbers are odd numbers.

   ....

   ....

   b) 5 is the only prime number that ends in the digit 5

   ....

   ....

   c) 109 is a prime number.

   ....

   .... **3 marks**

3. Write each number as the product of prime numbers only. One has been done for you.

   > Divide the numbers into factors. Then divide those into factors. Carry on until you cannot divide the numbers any further.

   a) $12 = 3 \times 4$
      $= 3 \times 2 \times 2$
   ....

   ....

   ....

   c) 25

   ....

   ....

   ....

   b) 56

   ....

   ....

   ....

   d) 72

   ....

   ....

   .... **3 marks**

Square numbers

1. Fill in the gaps. One has been done for you.

   a) ...6 × 6... $= 6^2$ $= $ ......36......

   b) .... $= 10^2$ $= $ ....

   c) .... $= 7^2$ $= $ ....

   d) 11 × 11 $= $ .... $= $ ....

   e) .... $= 3^2$ $= $ ....　　　　　　　　4 marks

2. Circle the square numbers.

   a) 33　　　64　　　13　　　25　　　121　　　9

   b) 27　　　38　　　16　　　4　　　22　　　14

   c) 35　　　42　　　81　　　144　　　12　　　36　　　3 marks

3. Match each number with its squared number. One has been done for you.

   8　　11　　7　　5　　10　　6

   121　25　36　64　49　100

   　　　　　　　　　　　　　　　　　　　　5 marks

4. An engineer is planning a wind farm. She puts the turbines in six rows. She puts six turbines in each row. How many turbines are there in the wind farm?

   ....

   ....　1 mark

5. A farmer sells eggs at the market in square trays. A tray holds 11 rows of 11 eggs. How many eggs can the farmer fit in each tray?

   ....

   ....　1 mark

15

Cube numbers

1. Fill in the gaps. One has been done for you.

   a) ...6 × 6 × 6... $= 6^3$ $= $ ...216...........

   b) $10 × 10 × 10 = $ .... $= $ ....

   c) $7 × 7 × 7$ $= $ .... $= $ ....

   d) .... $= 11^3$ $= $ ....

   e) .... $= 3^3$ $= $ ....   **4 marks**

2. Circle the cube numbers.

   a) 33   64   13   27   125   9

   b) 25   38   216   8   22   14

   c) 352   729   810   144   122   343   **3 marks**

3. Match each number with its cube number.

   2   7   4   8   10   100

   1,000,000   8   1,000   343   64   512   **2 marks**

4. A supermarket shelf has six tins of baked beans in a row. There are six rows on each shelf and six shelves. How many tins of baked beans are there in total?

   ....

   ....   **1 mark**

5. The multi-storey car park on Station Road has room for seven rows of cars with seven cars in each row. The car park is seven stories high.

   The multi-storey car park on Church Street has room for nine rows of cars with nine cars in each row. The car park is nine stories high.

   How many more cars can fit into the car park on Church Street than on Station Road?

   ....

   ....   **2 marks**

Short multiplication

1. Complete the calculations.

a) 545 × 4 =

```
    5 4 5
  ×     4
    1 2
  2 1 8 0      2,180
```
....

The first calculation has been done for you. Leave a line so that you have a space to move numbers into.

b) 835 × 9 =

....

c) 497 × 7 =

....

d) 2,550 × 5 =

....

3 marks

2. Complete the calculations by writing the correct numbers in the boxes.

a) 452 × 3 = 135☐

Look carefully at the place value to decide which number goes in the box.

b) 2,491 × 7 = ☐☐437

c) 643☐ × 4 = 2☐752

d) ☐.5 × 6 = 33

4 marks

3. A truck driver drives from Manchester to Rome and back again three times in one week. It is 1,378 miles from Manchester to Rome. How far did the truck travel in one week?

....   **1 mark**

Long multiplication

1. Complete the calculations. One has been done for you.

   a) 46 × 24 =

   b) 85 × 96 =

```
      4 6
   ×  2 4
   ─────────
   9¹2 0
   1 8²4
   1
   ─────────
   1 1 0 4
```
.....1,104.....

....

> Start by writing a 0 to show that the 2 means two 10s.

   c) 779 × 84 =

   d) 8,382 × 89 =

....

....

6 marks

2. How much money did each shop make?

   a) The computer game shop sold 8,476 games at £28 each.

> Use the written method to multiply the price by the number of items sold.

....

   b) The furniture shop sold 67 wardrobes at £286 each.

....

   c) The supermarket had 7,469 shoppers who spent £34 each.

....

6 marks

3. It is 3,459 miles from London to New York. A business executive flies there and back once every month. How many miles has she flown after a year?

....

4 marks

Short division

1. Complete the calculations.

   a) 5,244 ÷ 4 =

   b) 8,127 ÷ 9 =

The first example has been done for you.

```
      1 3 1 1
   4 ) 5¹2 4 4    1,311
```
....

   c) 2,550 ÷ 5 =

   d) 5,472 ÷ 3 =

....

3 marks

2. Use the signs < and > to show which is greater.

   a) 32 ÷ 4 ☐ 24 ÷ 8

   b) 208 ÷ 4 ☐ 436 ÷ 8

   c) 354 ÷ 6 ☐ 156 ÷ 3

   d) 5,454 ÷ 9 ☐ 4,840 ÷ 8

4 marks

3. The Nathoo family decides to buy a new car. They pay for the new car by making eight equal payments over two years. The cost of the car is £7,600. How much is each repayment?

.... **1 mark**

4. A construction company is building a new road at a safari park. The road will be 6,435 metres long. The company aims to build the road in 9 months. What length of road do they need to build every month to finish on time?

.... **1 mark**

19

Long division

1. Use long division to complete the calculations.

   a) $336 \div 24 =$

   ```
         1 4
   24)3 3 6      24
      2 4 0      48
        9 6      72
        9 6      96
          0     120     ..14..
   ```

   b) $481 \div 37 =$

   ....

   c) $814 \div 44 =$

   d) $7{,}906 \div 67 =$

   ....   **6 marks**

2. A farmer is packing 9,888 eggs into boxes. Each box will hold 24 eggs. How many boxes will the farmer need?

   ....   **2 marks**

3. Bhavik travels 3,682 miles in two weeks. If he travels the same distance each day, how far does he travel in one day?

   ....   **2 marks**

4. A teacher is cutting ribbon. He has 3,444 cm of ribbon to share equally among the 28 children in his class. What length of ribbon will each child get?

   ....   **4 marks**

Order of operations

1. Complete the calculations.

   a) $8 + 4 \times 9 =$ ....

   b) $80 \times 4 \div 2 =$ ....

   Do the multiplication and division first.

   c) $99 \div 3 + 7 - 35 =$ ....

   d) $(8 + 4) - 28 \div 4 =$ ....

   e) $(6 \times 5) \div (100 \div 10) =$ ....

   f) $20 \div (12 - 2) \times 60 =$ ....   6 marks

2. Add brackets to make the following statements true.

   a) $4 \times 3 + 2 = 20$

   b) $6 + 3 \times 2 - 14 \div 2 = 11$

   c) $5 + 5 \times 3 - 10 = 20$

   d) $6 \times 7 + 3 \div 2 + 1 = 31$

   e) $2 + 3 \times 7 - 2 = 25$ 5 marks

3. Pietro had £47 and Celia had £38. Pietro spent £15 and then gave half of the money he had left to charity. Use brackets to write a calculation that will tell you how much money Pietro and Celia have left altogether, then work out the answer.

   ....

   .... 1 mark

Solving problems

1. Here is a breakfast menu from a café. How much change will each person have from £10?

FOOD		DRINKS	
Full English breakfast	£6.50	Coffee	£3.30
Fruit teacake	£2.50	Tea	£2.75
Poached or scrambled egg on toast	£4.25	Herbal tea	£2.55
Scrambled egg and salmon on toast	£6.75	Orange, apple or cranberry juice	£1.75
Baked beans on toast	£4.55	Lemonade	£2.50

a) Tom chooses a full English breakfast and herbal tea.

....

....

b) Antanas chooses baked beans on toast and apple juice.

....

....

c) Abby chooses scrambled egg and salmon on toast with tea.

....

....

d) Maya chooses a fruit teacake and herbal tea.

....

.... 4 marks

2. A supermarket has 380 packets of pasta. 875 more packets are delivered. They are put on five shelves so that all the shelves have the same number of packets. How many packets of pasta are there on each shelf?

....

.... 2 marks

3. Ellie and Aisha bought some snacks at the cinema. Aisha bought a drink, some popcorn and a hot dog. Ellie bought a drink and some popcorn. Aisha paid £10.95 and Ellie paid £7.20. Popcorn costs £4.65. What is the cost of a drink? What is the cost of a hot dog?

....

.... 2 marks

Answering the question

1. A teacher is buying cakes for a class picnic. There are 27 children in the class and one packet contains 12 cakes. How many packets should the teacher buy to make sure that every child has at least two?

> There will be some cakes left over but the question asks 'How many packets?'

....   **2 marks**

2. A farmer is packing 5,580 cabbages into crates. Each crate holds 49 cabbages. How many crates can the farmer fill?

....   **1 mark**

3. The whole school is going on a trip to the beach. This is a list of the numbers of children and adults going on the trip.

class	number of children	number of adults
Reception	29	4
Yr1	30	3
Yr2	30	3
Yr3	28	2
Yr4	28	2
Yr5	30	2
Yr6	28	2

Each coach has room for 57 people, and coaches cost £350 each for the day.

How much will it cost to take the school to the beach?

....   **2 marks**

4. Mineral water is sold in packs of 6 bottles for £3.60, or packs of 4 bottles for £2.60. Which deal gives the better value?

....   **2 marks**

Fractions

1. What fraction of each diagram is shaded? What fraction is unshaded?

a)

b)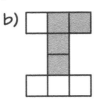

> The number of shaded sections plus the number of unshaded sections adds up to the total number of sections. The two fractions for each diagram should add up to one whole.

c)

d) ▭▭▭▭▭▭

a) shaded .... b) shaded ....

   unshaded ....   unshaded ....

c) shaded .... d) shaded ....

   unshaded ....   unshaded ....   **4 marks**

2. What do you notice about your answers to 1 c) and 1 d)?

.... **1 mark**

3. Shade each diagram by the fraction written next to it.

a) ▭▭▭▭▭ $= \frac{3}{5}$ b) (circle) $= \frac{7}{8}$ c) (grid) $= \frac{1}{3}$

3 marks

4. Jack had 36 sweets. He gave 12 to Joshua. What fraction of his sweets did he give to Joshua?

....

.... **2 marks**

24

Equivalent fractions

1. Write down two equivalent fractions to describe the shaded sections of each diagram.

   a)

   b)

   c)

   > First write down how many sections are shaded out of the total number, then simplify.

   .... and ....　　　　 .... and ....　　　　 .... and ....

   6 marks

2. Use multiples to find a pair of equivalent fractions with the same denominator. The first one has been started for you.

   a) $\frac{3}{4}$ and $\frac{2}{8}$ = $\frac{3}{4}$ and $\dfrac{\boxed{}}{4}$

   b) $\frac{2}{7}$ and $\frac{3}{5}$ = $\dfrac{\boxed{}}{35}$ and $\dfrac{\boxed{}}{35}$

   c) $\frac{2}{3}$ and $\frac{3}{4}$ = $\dfrac{\boxed{}}{\boxed{}}$ and $\dfrac{\boxed{}}{\boxed{}}$

   d) $\frac{1}{6}$ and $\frac{2}{5}$ = $\dfrac{\boxed{}}{\boxed{}}$ and $\dfrac{\boxed{}}{\boxed{}}$

   4 marks

3. Write each fraction in its simplest form. The first one has been started for you.

   a) $\frac{3}{12}$ = $\dfrac{\boxed{}}{4}$

   b) $\frac{12}{32}$ = $\dfrac{\boxed{}}{\boxed{}}$

   c) $\frac{21}{27}$ = $\dfrac{\boxed{}}{\boxed{}}$

   d) $\frac{48}{54}$ = $\dfrac{\boxed{}}{\boxed{}}$

   4 marks

4. James is doing his homework and has 80 questions to answer in total. So far, he has completed 16. What fraction of his homework has he completed, and what fraction does he still have left to do? Give your answers in their simplest form.

   ....

   ....　　 **2 marks**

Fractions greater than 1

1. Write each mixed number as an improper fraction.
   One has been done for you.

Always check to see if you can simplify your answer.

a) $6\frac{5}{8} = \frac{53}{8}$

b) $2\frac{12}{15} = \dots\dots$

c) $12\frac{2}{3} = \dots\dots$

d) $100\frac{3}{10} = \dots\dots$

e) $4\frac{4}{14} = \dots\dots$

f) $22\frac{10}{100} = \dots\dots$ **6 marks**

2. Write each improper fraction as a mixed number.
   One has been done for you.

a) $\frac{15}{8} = 1\frac{7}{8}$

b) $\frac{13}{12} = \dots\dots$

c) $\frac{101}{2} = \dots\dots$

d) $\frac{59}{27} = \dots\dots$

e) $\frac{46}{15} = \dots\dots$

f) $\frac{3}{2} = \dots\dots$ **6 marks**

3. After a party, Sanjay has 4 whole pies and $\frac{3}{4}$ of a pie left. He works out that if he slices the pies into quarters, each guest can have a slice to take home. How many guests are at his party?

....

....   **1 mark**

Comparing fractions

1. Use the symbol > or < to show which fraction is larger.

   a) $\dfrac{6}{8}$ ☐ $\dfrac{38}{76}$

   b) $\dfrac{253}{1000}$ ☐ $\dfrac{25}{100}$

   c) $\dfrac{14}{4}$ ☐ $\dfrac{9}{3}$

   > Look for common multiples for the denominators. Then multiply the numerator by the same number as the denominator.

   3 marks

2. Order the fractions on the number line.

   $\dfrac{12}{24}$　　$\dfrac{5}{6}$　　$\dfrac{2}{3}$　　$\dfrac{3}{8}$　　$\dfrac{3}{4}$　　$\dfrac{5}{12}$

   > Look for a common multiple and find equivalent fractions with the same denominator.

   0 ————————————————— 1

   6 marks

3. Padma and George are writing invitations to a party. They have the same number to write. Padma has written $\dfrac{7}{12}$ of hers and George has written $\dfrac{4}{7}$ of his. Who has written more?

   ....

   ....　　**1 mark**

4. Ruby and Harry each had a 100 g bar of chocolate. Ruby has $\dfrac{13}{16}$ left and Harry has $\dfrac{3}{4}$ left. Who has more chocolate?

   ....

   ....　　**1 mark**

Add/subtract fractions

1. Add the fractions.

a) $\frac{3}{12} + \frac{4}{12} =$ ....

b) $\frac{3}{7} + \frac{2}{5} =$ ....

c) $3\frac{5}{9} + 1\frac{5}{6} =$ ....

d) $\frac{13}{2} + \frac{15}{3} =$ ....

> To add fractions with different denominators, first change them to equivalent fractions with the same denominator.

4 marks

2. Subtract the fractions.

a) $\frac{9}{7} - \frac{4}{7} =$ ....

b) $\frac{4}{7} - \frac{2}{5} =$ ....

> Convert any answers which are improper fractions back to mixed fractions.

c) $3\frac{5}{9} - 1\frac{5}{6} =$ ....

d) $\frac{13}{2} - \frac{15}{3} =$ ....

4 marks

3. A bus is $4\frac{1}{3}$ metres tall. A bridge is $5\frac{7}{9}$ metres above the road.

How much space is there between the bus and the bridge?

....

.... **2 marks**

4. Luca and Cameron are carrying shopping from the supermarket.

They each carry 2 shopping bags. Luca's bags weigh $5\frac{4}{5}$ kg and $4\frac{1}{2}$ kg.

Cameron's bags weigh $4\frac{3}{10}$ kg and $5\frac{1}{2}$ kg.

Who is carrying the heavier amount?

How much more are they carrying?

....

....

.... **3 marks**

Multiplying fractions

1. Multiply each of these fractions by $\frac{1}{2}$, $\frac{1}{4}$ and $\frac{1}{8}$. The first one has been done for you.

fraction	$\times \frac{1}{2}$	$\times \frac{1}{4}$	$\times \frac{1}{8}$
$\frac{1}{3}$	$\frac{1}{6}$	$\frac{1}{12}$	$\frac{1}{24}$
$\frac{1}{5}$			
$\frac{1}{6}$			
$\frac{1}{7}$			

9 marks

2. Multiply the fractions.

a) $\frac{1}{6} \times \frac{1}{6} = $ ....

b) $\frac{3}{7} \times \frac{2}{5} = $ ....

c) $\frac{1}{3} \times \frac{3}{4} = $ ....

d) $\frac{3}{12} \times \frac{4}{12} = $ ....

e) $\frac{5}{10} \times \frac{5}{10} = $ ....

f) $\frac{10}{2} \times \frac{15}{3} = $ ....

> To multiply pairs of fractions multiply the numerators and multiply the denominators, then simplify the answer.

6 marks

3. Write two fractions that multiply together to make the given fraction.

a) $\frac{1}{4} = \dfrac{\square}{\square} \times \dfrac{\square}{\square}$

b) $\frac{1}{25} = \dfrac{\square}{\square} \times \dfrac{\square}{\square}$

c) $\frac{1}{8} = \dfrac{\square}{\square} \times \dfrac{\square}{\square}$

d) $\frac{2}{9} = \dfrac{\square}{\square} \times \dfrac{\square}{\square}$

> Find two factors of the numerator. Then find two factors of the denominator.

4 marks

Dividing fractions

1. Divide each of these fractions by 2, 3 and 4. The first one has been done for you.

fraction	÷ 2	÷ 3	÷ 4
$\frac{1}{3}$	$\frac{1}{6}$	$\frac{1}{9}$	$\frac{1}{12}$
$\frac{1}{5}$			
$\frac{1}{6}$			
$\frac{1}{7}$			

To divide a simple fraction by a whole number, multiply the denominator by the whole number to find the denominator of the result.

9 marks

2. Complete the following divisions.

a) $\frac{1}{12} \div 2 = $ ....

b) $\frac{1}{10} \div 6 = $ ....

c) $\frac{1}{2} \div 3 = $ ....

3 marks

3. Draw lines to match the equivalent amounts.

$\frac{1}{2} \div 3$ $\frac{1}{6} \div 3$ $\frac{1}{5} \div 3$ $\frac{1}{4} \div 3$

$\frac{1}{3} \div 6$ $\frac{1}{3} \div 4$ $\frac{1}{3} \div 2$ $\frac{1}{3} \div 5$ **4 marks**

4. Isabel shares a lasagne equally between two tables. The people on each table share their half equally. There are 4 people at the first table and 6 people at the second table. How much lasagne does each person at the first table get? How much does each person at the second table get?

First divide the lasagne between the tables, then divide it between the people at each table.

....

.... **2 marks**

Equivalent decimals and fractions

1. Fill in the gaps by writing fractions and decimals on the number line.

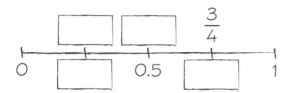

4 marks

2. Write a fraction and a decimal to describe the amount of each shape that has been shaded.

a)

 or ☐ . ☐

b)

☐/☐ or ☐ . ☐

c)

☐/☐ or ☐ . ☐

6 marks

3. Write the fractions as decimals.

a) $\dfrac{3}{12}$ = ...

b) $\dfrac{12}{24}$ = ...

c) $\dfrac{6}{30}$ = ...

d) $\dfrac{8}{64}$ = ...

4 marks

4. Write the decimals as fractions.

a) $0.5 = \dfrac{\square}{10}$

b) $0.25 = \dfrac{\square}{40}$

c) $0.2 = \dfrac{\square}{25}$

d) $0.75 = \dfrac{\square}{100}$

> Check the denominator to decide what the numerator should be.

4 marks

31

Multiplying decimals

1. Multiply each of these decimals by 10, 100 and 1,000. One has been done for you.

> To multiply by 10, 100 or 1,000, move the digits left by one, two or three places.

a) $0.65 \times 10 = $ ..6.5..

$0.65 \times 100 = $ ....

$0.65 \times 1,000 = $ ....

b) $9.25 \times 10 = $ ....

$9.25 \times 100 = $ ....

$9.25 \times 1,000 = $ ....

5 marks

2. Complete the calculations.

a) $0.35 \times 3 = $ ....

b) $6.22 \times 8 = $ ....

c) $3.51 \times 7 = $ ....

d) $8.02 \times 5 = $ ....   **4 marks**

3. Nadav is painting his shed. He works out that he needs 1.36 litres of paint for each coat. How much paint will he need for 3 coats?

....

....

....   **2 marks**

4. At a market, Celia buys 8 photo frames for £2.39 each. How much does she spend in total?

....

....

....   **2 marks**

Percentages

1. What percentage of the 100 square is shaded?
   What percentage is white?

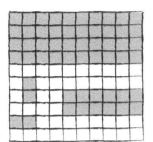

The way that the squares are arranged does not affect the amount or the percentage.

   a) shaded ....

   b) white ....

   2 marks

2. Use the cards to complete the number line.

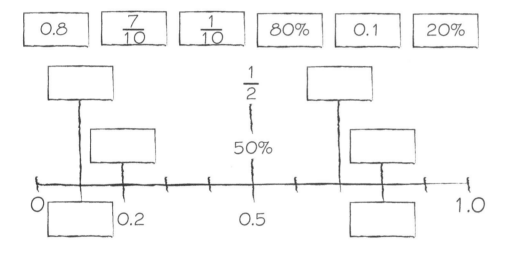

   6 marks

3. Max and Amelia shared a birthday cake. Max ate 30% of the cake and Amelia ate 20% of the cake. What percentage of the cake is left?

   ....

   .... **1 mark**

4. Five children share a pizza equally. What percentage of the pizza do they get each?

   ....

   .... **1 mark**

Converting percentages

1. Convert the percentages to fractions.
   One has been done for you.

   a) $20\% = \dfrac{1}{5}$

   b) $15\% = \dots\dots$

   c) $75\% = \dots\dots$

   d) $84\% = \dots\dots$

   e) $66\% = \dots\dots$

   f) $5\% = \dots\dots$

> Write the number as a fraction with 100 as the denominator, then simplify.

5 marks

2. Convert the following fractions to percentages.
   One has been done for you.

   a) $\dfrac{1}{4} = 25\%$

   b) $\dfrac{4}{10} = \dots\dots$

   c) $\dfrac{4}{5} = \dots\dots$

   d) $\dfrac{22}{50} = \dots\dots$

   e) $\dfrac{17}{25} = \dots\dots$

   f) $\dfrac{8}{20} = \dots\dots$

> Work out the equivalent decimal, then multiply by 100.

5 marks

3. 24 boys and 36 girls entered a talent show.
   What percentage of the entries were boys?

   ....

   ....

> Work out the total number of entries. Write 24 as the numerator and the total as the denominator. Then convert to a percentage.

2 marks

4. Jay has 40 marbles. $\dfrac{1}{4}$ of the marbles are green, $\dfrac{1}{5}$ of the marbles are red. The rest are blue.
   What percentage of the marbles are blue?

   ....

   ....

> Change the fractions to percentages. Subtract them from 100% to find out how many marbles are blue.

2 marks

Percentages of amounts

1. Work out these percentages.

   a) 20% of 60 = ...

   b) 50% of 95 = ...

   c) 25% of 160 = ...

   d) 75% of 200 = ...

   e) 10% of 320 = ...

   f) 30% of 120 = ...

> Once these percentages become familiar, you will be able to work them out in your head.

6 marks

2. Work out these percentages.

   a) 12% of 300 = ...

   b) 55% of 180 = ...

   c) 35% of 120 = ...

> Use facts such as '5% is half of 10%' to find the amounts you need.

3 marks

3. A chocolate bar has 20 pieces. Chloe eats 3 pieces and Jal eats 4 pieces. What percentage of the chocolate bar is left?

   ....

   ....   **2 marks**

4. There are 250 children in school. 60% have school dinners, 30% have packed lunches and 10% go home for lunch.

   a) How many children have a school dinner?

   ....

   ....

   b) How many children have a packed lunch?

   ....

   ....

   c) How many children go home for lunch?

   ....

   ....   **3 marks**

Solving percentage problems

1. A class took a test with 50 questions. The percentage of questions each pupil answered correctly is given below. How many questions did each pupil get right? The first one has been done for you.

   a) Antti $100\% = \dfrac{50}{50}$ **b)** Anna $60\% = \dfrac{\square}{50}$

   c) James $70\% = \dfrac{\square}{50}$ **d)** Hannah $50\% = \dfrac{\square}{50}$

3 marks

2. At a birthday party, a cake is cut into 20 pieces and 80% are eaten. How many pieces of cake are left?

....

....   1 mark

3. Circle the greater amount of money.

   a) 45% of £40 or 20% of £120

   b) 80% of £200 or 50% of £300

   c) 10% of £50 or 70% of £10

   d) 5% of £100,000 or 99% of £4,999

4 marks

4. Nabil has 120 toy cars. Ava has 20 toy cars. 10% of Nabil's cars are blue. 90% of Ava's cars are blue. Who has more blue cars?

....

....   1 mark

Ratio

1. Write the ratios below each diagram.

grey : white   grey : white

...3..:..2..   ...7..:..3..

2 marks

2. Colour the squares to make each ratio correct.

a) 1 coloured : 5 white

b) 4 coloured : 2 white

2 marks

3. When making cordial, Padma needs to add 4 measures of water for every 1 measure of cordial. What is this as a ratio?

....

> A ratio compares the amount of each part within the whole.

1 mark

4. On a pool table, there are 7 red balls, 4 yellow balls and 1 white ball. What is the ratio of red balls to balls that are not red?

....

....

1 mark

5. To make meringue, Rosie whisked 160 g of egg white with 240 g of sugar.

What was the ratio of egg white to sugar? Write the ratio in its simplest form.

> Just like fractions, ratios can be simplified.

....

....

2 marks

Proportion

1. Here are some shaded tiles.

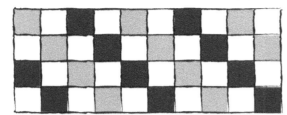

> When talking about proportions, use the phrase 'out of'. You can write proportions as fractions.

What proportion of the tiles are:

a) black? ......

b) grey? ......

c) white? ......

> Just like fractions, proportions should be written in their simplest form.

3 marks

2. A bag contains 64 grapes. There are 16 red grapes and 48 white grapes.
   What proportion are:

   a) red grapes? ....

   b) white grapes? ....

2 marks

3. There are 27 children in Year Six. 12 are boys and 15 are girls.
   What proportion of the class are:

   a) boys? ....   b) girls? ....

2 marks

4. On a farm there are 10 hens, 30 sheep and 60 cows.
   What proportion of the animals are:

   a) hens? ....

   b) sheep? ....

   c) cows? ....

3 marks

Scale factors

1. This triangle has been enlarged by a scale factor of 2. What are the new measurements of the sides A, B and C?

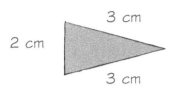

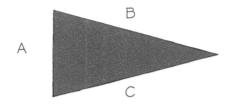

Always use the same side in similar shapes to work out the scale factor.

A = ……….. cm   B = ……….. cm   C = ……….. cm

3 marks

2. A regular hexagon has equal sides of 3 cm. It is enlarged to have equal sides of 21 cm. What scale factor was used to enlarge the hexagon?

……………………………………………………………………………………   **1 mark**

3. This trapezium has sides of length:

   A = 2 cm   B = 3 cm   C = 4 cm

Complete the table to show the lengths of the sides after they are enlarged by different scale factors.

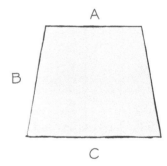

scale factor	A	B	C
2	4 cm		
5			20 cm
10		30 cm	
$\frac{1}{2}$			2 cm

4 marks

4. A chocolate bar is 10 cm long. The 'family size' version is $1\frac{1}{2}$ times longer. How long is the 'family size' chocolate bar?

……………………………………………………………………………………

……………………………………………………………………………………   **1 mark**

Unequal sharing and grouping

1. Here are 35 buttons. Put them in 2 groups in the ratio of 2:3 by drawing a ring around each group.

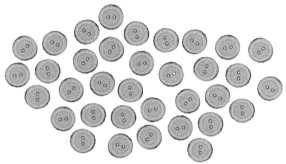

> The ratio parts add together to make 5. One group should have $\frac{2}{5}$ of the counters and the other group should have $\frac{3}{5}$

1 mark

2. Evie is making piles of cubes in the ratio of 4 yellow cubes for every 1 red cube. There are 25 cubes altogether. How many yellow cubes are there and how many red cubes are there?

....

.... **1 mark**

3. £160 is shared among 2 people using the ratio 3:5. How much money do they get each?

> The parts of the ratio add up to 8. Look for multiples of 8

....

....

1 mark

4. In a class there are 2 boys for every 3 girls. There are 15 girls in the class. How many boys are there?

> Keep the ratio the same. To get from 3 girls to 15 you multiply by 5, so do the same for the boys.

....

....

1 mark

Ratio problems

1. Fudge is made with butter, milk and sugar in the following ratios.

butter : sugar   2 : 9   butter : milk   2 : 3

Complete the table to show how much of each ingredient would be needed to make the following amounts of fudge.

butter (g)	sugar (g)	milk (ml)
100	450	
		300
1,000		
	225	

7 marks

2. These are the ingredients needed to make one 150 ml bottle of vanilla shower gel.

120 g liquid soap
25 g vegetable glycerine
5 g vanilla extract

a) Emma has 80 g of liquid soap. How many millilitres of shower gel can she make?

....

....   **2 marks**

b) Alan has 300 g of liquid soap, 65 g of glycerine and 15 g of vanilla extract. How many full bottles of shower gel can he make?

....

....   **2 marks**

3. 2 people share £4,800 in the ratio of 2 : 3
How much do they get each?

....

....   **2 marks**

Using letters

5⟌55

1. Find the value of the letter in each number sentence.

a) $d - 11 = 89$ ..d = 100......................................

b) $f \times 5 = 55$ ..f = 11...

c) $h \div 7 = 9$ ..h = 63...

d) $b + 3 = 31$ ..b = 28...

4 marks

2. Monty thinks of a number and multiplies it by 4. The answer is 24.
What is the number Monty thought of?

....

....

....

> Use inverse operations.
>
> | operation | + | − | × | ÷ |
> |---|---|---|---|---|
> | inverse | − | + | ÷ | × |

1 mark

3. You have forgotten the code for your bike lock. Fortunately, you wrote
down some clues to help you remember. Work out the value of
each letter to find your code.

> 2a means
> 2 × a

clue	$2a = 18$	$\dfrac{b}{3} = 3$	$c - 4 = 5$	$d + 7 = 11$
show your working				
code				

4 marks

4. Hannah thinks of a number, adds 12 and then
subtracts 9. The answer is 50.

What is the number Hannah thought of?

> Work backwards
> from 50
> using inverse
> operations.

....

....

2 marks

Simple formulae

Kasim is selling his old video games to his friends. He uses this formula to work out how much to charge in pounds.

cost = number of games × £4 + 25p for each instruction booklet

1. How much will 5 games cost without any instruction booklets?

....   1 mark

2. How much will 7 games and 2 instruction booklets cost?

....

....

> Work out the cost of the games and the cost of the instructions and add them together.

2 marks

3. Kasim's friend Jeremy buys four games and some instruction booklets. He pays Kasim a total of £16.75.

   How many instruction booklets does he buy?

....

....   1 mark

4. Another friend spends £8.50. She buys two instruction booklets. How many games does she buy?

....   1 mark

Linear sequences

1. Complete this sequence.

   3,   10, ...,   24, ..., ...,   45, ...,   59

   +7   +7   +7   +7   +7   +7   +7   +7

   1 mark

2. a) Complete this sequence.

   38, ...,   28,   23, ...,   13, ..., ...

   1 mark

   b) What is the term-to-term rule for this sequence?

   ....

   ....

   > Look at the two terms that are next to each other to work out the how much is being subtracted each time.

   1 mark

3. Complete this sequence.

   7,   11, ...   19,   23, ..., ..., ...,   39

   1 mark

4. The first term of a sequence is 19. The rule is add 6 to the previous term. Write the first six terms of this sequence.

   ....

   ....

   1 mark

5. The fifth term of a linear sequence is 25. The rule is add 5 to the previous term. What is the first term?

   ....

   ....

   ....

   > Use the inverse operation to work back from the fifth to the first term.

   1 mark

Two unknowns

1. What pair of numbers less than 10 could be hidden under the counters?
   Think of three possible answers.

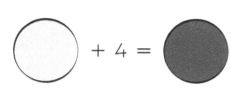

white = ...　　　　black = ...

white = ...　　　　black = ...

white = ...　　　　black = ...

3 marks

2. p and q are positive integers that are less than 9. List all the possible
   numbers they could be for each equation.

	$p + 6 = q$	$q - 3 = p$	$p - 5 = q$	$q + 7 = p$
possible number pairs for p and q				

4 marks

3. Keri is trying to work out the possible answers to
   this formula: $m + 7 - 2 = n$

   She knows that m and n are positive integers less
   than 10. She thinks that m could be 4 and n
   could be 8.

   > Your explanation must
   > include an example
   > using the numbers
   > given and say what
   > this proves.

   Is Keri correct?　　　　　　yes ☐　　no ☐

   Explain how you know.

   ....

   ....

   ....　　**2 marks**

Combination problems

1. Frankie likes 4 types of footwear: boots, sandals, trainers and wellies. He buys each type in three different colours: black, brown and green. Complete the table of combinations.

Which type of footwear must be in the last column?

black		black trainers	
	brown sandals		
green boots			

4 marks

2. Harriet loves a cup of tea, coffee or hot chocolate. Sometimes she adds milk, sugar or cream. Draw a table of the combinations of drink she could have.

Use multiplication to work out the number of combinations.

1 mark

3. The Year 6 girls are playing the Year 6 boys in a netball match. The final score is 2–2. What could the half-time score have been? List all the possible scores.

Work through one by one so you don't miss any out.

....

....

2 marks

4. In a field, there are some farmers and some sheep. The total number of legs is 100. What combination of farmers and sheep could be in the field? List 3 possible combinations.

Don't forget that farmers and sheep have different numbers of legs!

....

....

....

3 marks

Algebra problems

1. Ben has two types of coin. The totals of each row and column are shown in pence. Find the value of each coin.

○ + ◇ = 22p   ○ = ... p

○ + ○ = 4p   ◇ = ... p

◇ + ◇ = 40p

> Look for two of the same symbols in a row to start off.

5 marks

2. The perimeter of a rectangular picture is 45 cm. It is twice as long as it is high. What is the height (*h*) and length (*l*) of the picture?

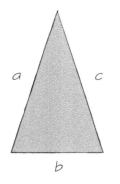

height

length

> Think about how many times the height fits into the perimeter.

....

....   **2 marks**

3. The perimeter of an isosceles triangle measures 21 cm. The side labelled *a* is 9 cm long. How long is the side labelled *b*?

a   *c*   Not to scale

b

> In an isosceles triangle, two sides are always the same length.

....

....   **2 marks**

Reading scales

1. Look at the readings for each of these scales. Are they true or false?

	reading	true	false
(thermometer scale −5° 0° 5°)	−6 °C		
(grams scale 100 200 300 400 500 600 700 800)	475 g		
(centimetres/feet scale)	45 cm is approximately $1\frac{1}{2}$ feet		

3 marks

2. This diagram shows the volumes of orange juice in two measuring jugs.

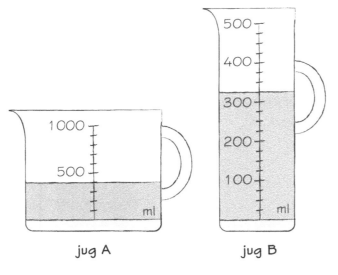

jug A   jug B

Look carefully at the scales on the two jugs.

Which jug contains less juice?

A ☐   B ☐

Explain how you know.

....

....   2 marks

Converting units

1. Yasmina has converted some measurements.

   Decide whether each conversion is correct or incorrect. If a conversion is incorrect, write the correct answer in the final column.

   > Check that Yasmina has moved the digits the correct number of places each time.

	correct	incorrect	write the correct answer here
7.2 m = 7200 cm			
65 mm = 6.5 cm			
1160 g = 11.60 kg			
0.25 litres = 250 ml			

4 marks

2. Duncan is mixing plaster. He needs 500 g of powder and 230 ml of water.

   a) He takes the powder from a 2 kg packet. How much powder is left in the packet in grams?

   > You will need to convert from kg to g and l to ml.

   ....

   b) He takes the water from a half-litre bottle. How much water is left in the bottle in millilitres?

   ....

   2 marks

3. Each wing of a model aeroplane is 5.5 cm long. The body is 35 mm wide. What is the total wingspan of the model in millimetres?

   > The wingspan is the distance from wingtip to wingtip including the body of the aeroplane.

   ....

   ....

   ....

   3 marks

Ordering measures

1. Draw a line to match each measurement to its equivalent amount.

> Make sure you know the relationship between the units and how to convert.

15 cm	150 cm	0.9 litres	6.5 kg	90 litres	0.650 kg

1.5 m	650 g	90,000 ml	150 mm	900 ml	6,500 g

2. Look at each of these comparisons. Is it true or false?

a) 2,100 mm is longer than 21 cm.   true ☐   false ☐

b) 6,200 g is heavier than $6\frac{1}{4}$ kg.   true ☐   false ☐

c) $\frac{3}{4}$ litres is a smaller capacity than 800 ml.   true ☐   false ☐   **3 marks**

3. Look at each of these comparisons. Insert < or > between the measures.

a) 200 cm ☐ 20 m

b) 4,000 g ☐ 75 kg

c) 500 ml ☐ 0.05 litres

d) $\frac{1}{2}$ km ☐ 5,000 mm

e) 1,050 g ☐ 1.5 kg

f) 9 litres ☐ 900 ml

> < means less than and > means more than.

3 marks

4. Put these measures in order of size, smallest to largest.

a) 2 km, 2,500 m, 2,050 m, 2,100 cm

> Look carefully at the units.

....

b) 1,250 ml, 1.255 litres, 1,350 ml, 1,025 ml

....

c) 0.1 kg, 15,000 g, 1,500 g, 10 g

....   **3 marks**

Imperial units

1. One pint is about 500 ml. Leila's mum orders 6 pints of milk to be delivered. How many litres of milk does she order?

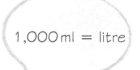

1,000 ml = litre

....

1 mark

2. Neil weighs 140 pounds.

   a) There are 14 pounds in 1 stone. How much does Neil weigh in stone?

   ....

   b) One stone is about 6 kg. How much does Neil weigh in kilograms?

   ....

2 marks

3. Lara's friend is visiting from France, where distances are given in *kilometres*. Her friend wants to know the distances to the nearest towns. Here is a table of distance in *miles*.

Convert from miles to kilometres by multiplying by 1.6

	Gloucester	Cheltenham	Bristol
Gloucester	–	10	50
Cheltenham	10	–	60
Bristol	50	60	–

   a) How far is it from Gloucester to Cheltenham in kilometres?

   ....

   ....

   b) How far is a round trip from Gloucester to Bristol in kilometres?

   ....

A round trip means travelling there and back.

   ....

4 marks

Measure calculations

1. Convert these measures.

a) 560 g = ...0.56... kg

b) 0.98 m = ... cm

c) 1.77 litres = ... ml

d) 45 mm = ... cm

e) 0.63 kg = ... g

f) 920 cm = ... m

> 1 m = 100 cm
> 1 cm = 10 mm
> 1 litre = 1,000 ml
> 1 kg = 1,000 g

5 marks

2. Calculate the following. Use an appropriate written method.

> Convert all measurements to the same units before you calculate.

a) Charlie adds 360 g of sugar to 0.42 kg of butter. What is the total weight of his mixture in grams?

....

b) A robot travels in a straight line forward 210 cm and then reverses 0.5 m. How far has it travelled from the start in centimetres?

....

c) Shannon has 5 floor tiles, each 125 cm long. She lays them down end to end. What is the total length of the tiles in metres?

....

d) Sabina and her two brothers share 2.1 litres of juice. What volume of juice does each person get in millilitres?

....   **8 marks**

Time

1. Convert these units of time. One has been done for you.

   a) 130 seconds → ..2.. minutes and .10.. seconds

   b) $3\frac{1}{2}$ hours → .... minutes

   c) 109 weeks → .... years and ....weeks

   d) 20 decades → .... centuries

> 52 weeks = 1 year
> 10 years = 1 decade
> 100 years = 1 century

                                                          3 marks

2. Write these analogue times in 24-hour form. One has been done for you.

   a) half-past ten in the morning → 10:30

   b) quarter to nine in the evening → ....

   c) twenty-five past midnight → ....   **4 marks**

3. Here are some low tide and high tide times for a weekend in June.

date	1st low tide	1st high tide	2nd low tide	2nd high tide
Friday 7th	02:43	09:02	15:08	21:53
Saturday 8th	03:21	09:44	15:44	22:05
Sunday 21th	03:58	10:27	16:23	22:48

   a) How many minutes later is the 1st low tide on Sunday than on Friday?

> The tide comes in and goes out twice a day.

   ....

                                                           1 mark

   b) You are on the beach on the Saturday evening. You check your watch.

> Work out the difference between the two times in hours and minutes, then convert to minutes only.

   How many minutes is it until the next high tide?

   ....   **2 marks**

Perimeter and area

1. Work out the areas and perimeters of these rectangles.

    a) length = 6 cm   →   area = ...30... cm²,
        width = 5 cm   perimeter = ...22... cm

    b) length = 12 cm   →   area = ... cm²,
        width = 4 cm   perimeter = ... cm

    c) length = 21 m   →   area = ... m²,
        width = 3 m   perimeter = ... m

    d) length = 10 mm   →   area = ... mm
        width = 2.5 mm   perimeter = ... mm

    > Remember that area = l x w and perimeter = 2 x (l + w).

    3 marks

2. The area of a rectangle is 20 cm². One of the sides is 2 cm long.

    What is the perimeter of the rectangle?

    ...The perimeter of the rectangle is 40 cm²
    20 × 2 = 40...

    > Work out the length of the other sides.

    1 mark

3. Gareth has some star-shaped tiles. Each edge is 4 cm long.

    He puts two tiles together to make this shape:

    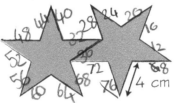

    4 cm

    Work out the perimeter of Gareth's shape.

    ...The perimeter would be ~~76cm²~~ 72cm²
    and because the two stars
    are connecting it would be ~~76~~ 72cm²

    > Go all the way around the new shape and make sure you only count each side once.

    2 marks

Compound shapes

1. A smaller rectangle has been removed from this shape.

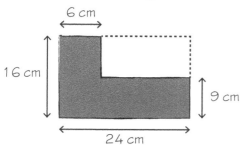

Find the unknown lengths and use the perimeter formula.

Find the perimeter of the missing rectangle.

....

....   **2 marks**

2. Anastasia has three rectangles of the same size. They have a length of 9 cm and a height of 4 cm. She puts them together to make this shape.

What is the perimeter of Anastasia's compound shape?

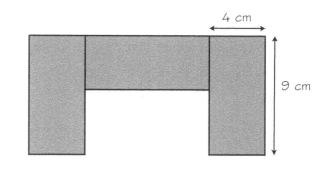

....

....

....   **3 marks**

3. Here is a design for a flag.

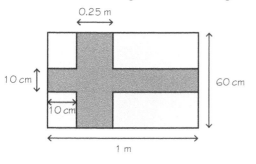

Convert all the measurements to the same unit. Make sure you count all the sides.

Calculate the perimeter of the shaded cross shape.

....

....

....   **3 marks**

Areas of triangles

1. Here are three triangles on a 1 cm by 1 cm grid.

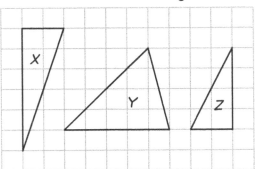

> Make sure you count the base and height lengths on the grids carefully.

a) What is the area of triangle X?

.... **1 mark**

b) What is the difference in area between the triangle with the smallest area and the triangle with the largest area?

> Use the formula $\frac{1}{2}$ (base x height)

....

....

2 marks

2. Steven is asked to calculate the total area of the two playgrounds at his school. He works out that the total is 550 m².

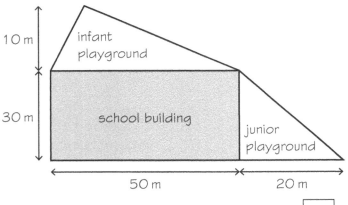

> Use the dimensions of the school building to help you and add together the areas of both playgrounds.

Is his calculation correct?   Yes ☐   No ☐

Explain how you know.

....

....

.... **2 marks**

Areas of parallelograms

1. Calculate the area of each parallelogram.

   a) base length = 15 cm

   perpendicular height = 6 cm

   ....

   b) base length = 0.21 m

   perpendicular height = 0.1 m

   ....

> area = base length x perpendicular height

> Convert from metres to centimetres before calculating.

2 marks

2. Use the grid below to draw a parallelogram with the same area as this rectangle.

> Make sure your shape has two pairs of equal opposite parallel sides.

2 marks

3. Han has some parallelogram-shaped tiles as shown below. He puts three together to make a new shape. What is the total area of his new shape?

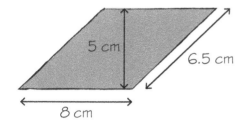

5 cm   6.5 cm   8 cm

> Remember to give the units of your answer.

....

....   **2 marks**

57

Volumes of cuboids

1. Calculate the volume of each cuboid.

> Volume = $l \times w \times h$

a) length = 2 m; width = 3 m; height = 6 m

2x3=6. 6x6=36. 36cm³

b) length = 30 mm; width = 30 mm; height = 10 mm

> Remember to use the correct units in your answers.

30x30=900. 900x10=9000. 9000mm³

c) length = 5 cm; width = 5 cm; height = 5 cm

5x5=25. 25x5=125. 125cm³

3 marks

(margin working:)
30x
30
─────
00 +
900
900
900x
102
000 +
9000
9000

25 x
5
─────
25
2

2. Tobias is making shapes from centimetre cubes.

a) The first shape he makes looks like this. How many more centimetre cubes does he need to make a solid cuboid 4 cm long, 4 cm wide and 3 cm tall?

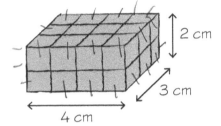

2 cm
3 cm
4 cm

20 It would be 20 cm

2 marks

b) The second shape he makes is a solid cuboid with a volume of 30 cm³.

What could its length, height and width be?

length .... cm

width .... cm

height .... cm

> Remember you are multiplying to find the volume, not adding.

1 mark

2D shape properties

1. Sunta describes the properties of some mystery 2D shapes. Name the shapes she is describing.

   a) "This shape has 3 equal sides and 3 equal angles."

   ....   1 mark

   b) "This shape is regular. It has 4 pairs of equal opposite parallel sides."

   How many sides must this shape have altogether?

   ....

      1 mark

2. Here are four shapes on a square grid.

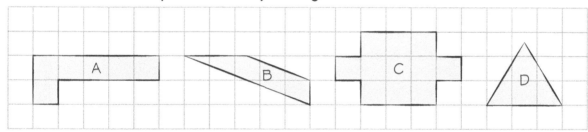

   a) Write the letter of each shape that is regular.   ....

   b) Write the letter of each shape that has a line of symmetry.   ....

   c) Write the letter of each shape that has 3 or more equal angles. ....

      5 marks

3. Draw two straight lines across the octagon to make one triangle, one quadrilateral and one pentagon. Each shape must be irregular.

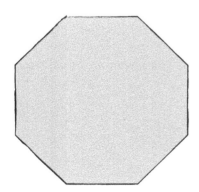

   There are lots of ways of doing this. Use a ruler to draw straight lines between the corners.

      1 mark

Naming 2D shapes

1. Circle the correct name for each quadrilateral. One has been done for you.

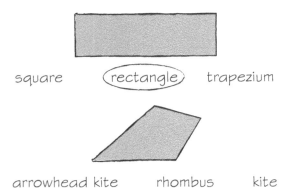

square   (rectangle)   trapezium

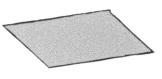

trapezium   rhombus   parallelogram

arrowhead kite   rhombus   kite

trapezium   parallelogram   kite

3 marks

2. Label these triangles 'equilateral', 'isosceles' or 'scalene' and complete their properties. One has been done for you.

equilateral
__3__ equal sides and __3__ equal angles

_____ equal sides and _____ equal angles

_____ equal sides and _____ equal angles

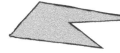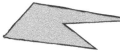

_____ equal sides and _____ equal angles

3 marks

3. Are these shapes regular or irregular? Tick the correct box for each shape

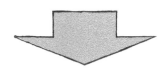

regular ☐   irregular ☐   regular ☐   irregular ☐

> Regular means that all the sides are equal and all the angles are the same.

regular ☐   irregular ☐   regular ☐   irregular ☐

4 marks

Naming 3D shapes

1. Circle the correct names and properties for these 3D shapes. One has been done for you.

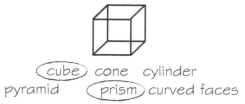

cube   cone   cylinder
pyramid   prism   curved faces

square pyramid   tetrahedron   cuboid
pyramid   prism   curved faces

cone   triangular prism   sphere
pyramid   prism   curved faces

tetrahedron   pentagonal prism   cone
pyramid   prism   curved faces

3 marks

2. Flora places a cuboid on top of another cuboid like this:

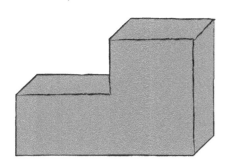

> Remember to count the faces, vertices and edges you can't see.

Flora's shape has ...... faces, ... vertices and ...... edges.   **2 marks**

3. Complete this table.

shape	faces	vertices	edges
cuboid	6		
square pyramid			8
cylinder		0	

3 marks

Nets

1. These nets fold to make 3D shapes. Match each net to the name of the 3D shape. One has been done for you.

A prism has a pair of faces that are the same shape.

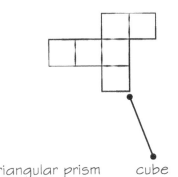  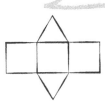

triangular prism   cube   tetrahedron   cylinder   octahedron   square pyramid

3 marks

2. A cube has shaded squares on three of its faces. Look at the drawing of the cube and shade the net to show where the shaded squares would be.

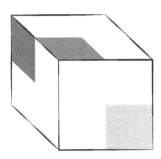 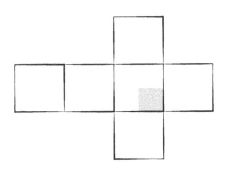

2 marks

3. Look at this pentagonal prism and its net. Draw the two missing faces that complete the net for this 3D shape.

Imagine folding up this net. Which faces would be missing?

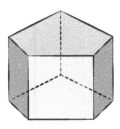 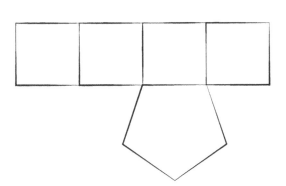

2 marks

Angles

1. Here are some angles measured in degrees. Are they acute, obtuse or reflex?

   a) 70° ....acute.....

   c) 169° ....obtuse....

   b) 290° ....Reflex.......

   d) 185° ....Reflex......

   4 marks

2. Circle the correct label for each angle. One has been done for you.

   a) acute   (obtuse)   reflex

   b) acute   obtuse   (reflex)

   c) acute   (obtuse)   reflex

   d) (acute)   obtuse   reflex

   3 marks

3. Use a protractor to measure the labelled angles in this quadrilateral and complete the table.

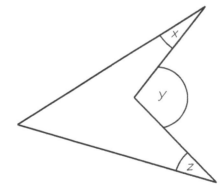

   Estimate each angle by eye before you measure with a protractor.

angle	size of angle	type of angle
x	°	
y	°	
z	°	

   4 marks

Calculating angles

1. Fill in the missing angles.

    a) angles in a triangle   30° + ...**100**...° + 50° = ...**180**...°

    b) angles about a point   180° + ...° + 80° = ...°

    c) angles along a straight line   15° + ...° + 120° = ...°

    d) angles in a quadrilateral   ....° + 90° + 25° + 45° = ...°

4 marks

2. Work out the unknown angles. The diagrams are not drawn to scale.

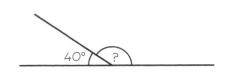 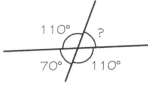 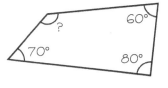

         ....°   ....°

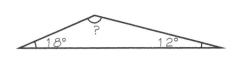 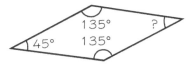 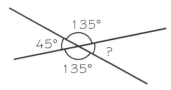

.........°   ....°   ....°

3 marks

3. Find the value of x.

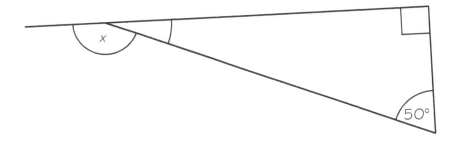

> Work out the unknown angle inside the triangle first.

....

....

....

2 marks

Drawing 2D shapes

1. Draw a scalene triangle, using the line below as one of the sides. The side on the left should be 6 cm long and should make an angle of 52° to the side that has already been drawn.

10 cm

> You can use a protractor and a ruler to help draw the shape.

2 marks

2. Here is a sketch of a quadrilateral. It is not drawn to scale.
   Draw the full-size quadrilateral accurately.
   Two lines have been done for you.

> You will need to use a ruler with millimetre markings.

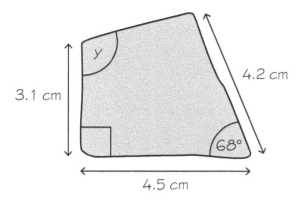

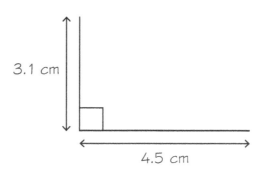

2 marks

3. What is the size of angle y in your drawing?

.... **1 mark**

Circles

1. Write down which feature has been marked on each of these circles.

a)    b) 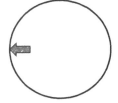   c)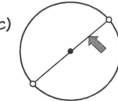

> The diameter is twice the length of the radius.

....   **4 marks**

2. Billy has drawn a circle and measured the radius, diameter and the circumference but he has muddled up his measurements. Draw lines to match each measurement to the right feature.

5.8 cm	circumference
18.2 cm	radius
2.9 cm	diameter

1 mark

3. Three large circles and four small circles fit exactly inside this rectangle.

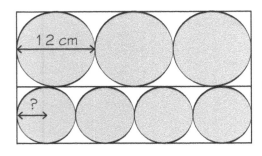

12 cm

?

not actual size

> To start, calculate the total diameter of the three large circles.

The diameter of a large circle is 12 cm.
Calculate the radius of a small circle.

....

....

....   **2 marks**

Coordinates

1. Here is a trapezium on a coordinate grid.

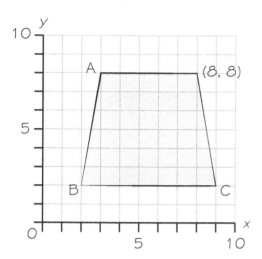

It might help you to label the missing numbers on the axes before you try to read the coordinates.

What are the coordinates of A, B and C?

A is at (...... , ...)   B is at (...... , ...)   C is at (...... , ...) **3 marks**

2. A square has vertices at (8, 3), (8, 8) and (3, 8). What are the coordinates of its last vertex?

.... **2 marks**

3. M, N and P are three corners of a rectangle.

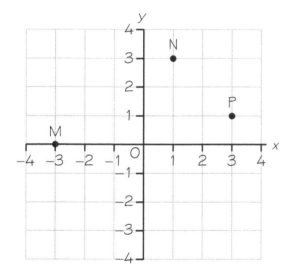

Draw lines to join up the corners you know to help you visualise the shape.

What are the coordinates of the fourth corner?

(...... , ...) **1 mark**

Translations

1. Here is a quadrilateral ABCD on a four-quadrant coordinate grid.

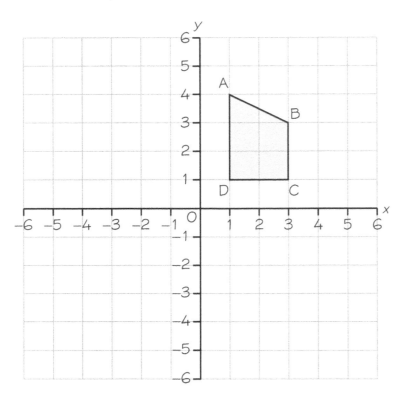

a) The quadrilateral is translated 5 squares to the left and
6 squares down. A is now at (−4, −2). Draw the translated
shape on the grid.   **2 marks**

b) What are the new coordinates of B, C and D?

B is at (......... , ...)   C is at (......... , ...)   D is at (......... , ...)

     3 marks

c) From its new position, the quadrilateral is now translated 4 to the right and
2 squares up.

What are the new coordinates of A, B, C and D?

A is at (......... , ...)

B is at (......... , ...)

C is at (......... , ...)

D is at (......... , ...)

You could answer
this question using
addition. Add 4 to
the x-coordinate
and add 2 to the
y-coordinate.

     4 marks

Reflection

1. Reflect the shape on the grid in the mirror line.

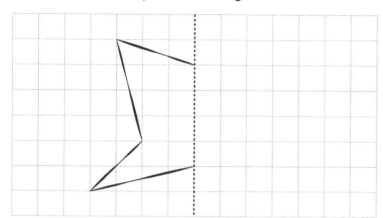

> Think of the mirror line like the *y*-axis. The shape will not move up or down.

1 mark

2. Here is a triangle on a four-quadrant coordinate grid.

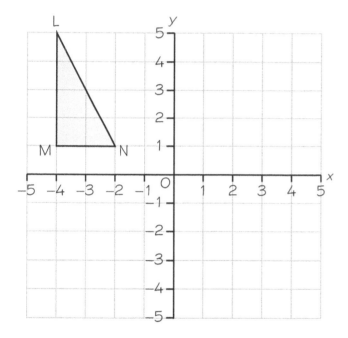

The triangle is reflected in the x-axis, and then from its new position it is reflected in the y-axis.

a) Draw the reflected shape on the grid.

> Draw both the reflected shapes on the grid making sure to reflect them in the correct axes.

1 mark

b) The final coordinates of L are (4, −5).

What are the final coordinates of M and N?

M is at (…….. , ………)　　　　　　　N is at (…….. , ………)　　　**2 marks**

Tables

1. Here is a famous sentence that contains all the letters in the English alphabet. Some letters are used more than once.

> Make sure the total frequency matches the total number of letters in the sentence.

The quick brown fox jumps over the lazy dog.

a) Tally up the groups of letters and complete the table (the letters **k** to **o** have been done for you).

group of letters	tally	frequency
a–e (a b c d e)		
f–j (f g h i j)		
k–o (k l m n o)	ⅼⅼⅼⅼ ⅼⅼⅼ	8
p–t (p q r s t)		
u–z (u v w x y z)		

b) Which group of letters occurs most frequently? ....

c) Which group of letters has a frequency of 7? ....

d) How many times do the letters from **a** to **j** occur? ....

4 marks

2. Hamish is catching the bus into the centre of town to go to the cinema. This is the timetable at the bus stop.

Ramsey Road	10:30	10:50	11:10	11:30	11:50	then every 30 mins
Huntley Way	10:37	10:57	11:17	11:37	11:57	then every 30 mins
Leisure Centre	10:49	▨	11:29	11:49	12:09	then every 30 mins
Central Bus Station	11:02	11:22	11:42	12:02	12:22	then every 30 mins

a) How many minutes does the journey from Ramsey Road to the Central Bus Station take? ....

b) The ink has smudged on one of the times. What is the missing time? ....

c) The film starts at 12:15. What time is the latest bus from Huntley Way that Hamish can catch to get there on time? ....

d) Hamish decides to take the 11:17 bus. He phones his friends who are at the leisure centre to tell them to get on the same bus. What time does he tell his friends the bus will arrive? ....

4 marks

Bar charts

1. Some classes took part in a sponsored swim. Here is a chart showing how many lengths each class completed.

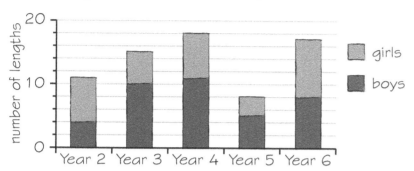

Write the missing numbers on the vertical axis to help you read the chart accurately.

a) How many lengths did the boys swim in Year 6? .... **1 mark**

b) How many more lengths did Year 3 swim than Year 5? .... **1 mark**

c) At the end of the swim, the head teacher announced that in total, the boys swam 7 more lengths than the girls. Was the head correct? Write down how you know.

yes ☐   no ☐

....

.... **2 marks**

2. Connie surveys her class to see what genres of book her classmates are reading.

genre	number of books
adventure	15
autobiography	9
horror	5
comedy	12

This bar chart shows the information from the table. Connie has forgotten to draw one of the bars.

a) Fill in all the missing labels on the horizontal axis and vertical axis.

b) Draw the missing bar.

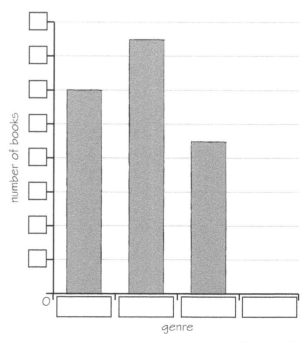

3 marks

71

Pie charts

1. This chart shows the favourite fruit of the children in a Year 6 class.

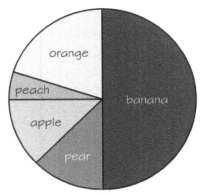

a) What fraction of the children liked bananas the most? .... **1 mark**

b) There are 28 children in the class.

How many children preferred bananas, pears or apples? ....

.... **2 marks**

2. A group of 60 children in Year 4 were asked what they thought was their worst habit in class.

Here are the results for the boys and the girls.

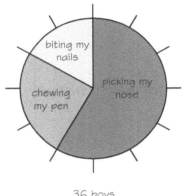

36 boys

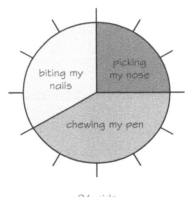

24 girls

> Be careful. The number of girls and boys is different.

a) How many boys said 'chewing my pen'? .... **1 mark**

b) How many girls said 'biting my nails'? .... **1 mark**

c) Kumar claims that more girls than boys pick their noses.

Is he correct? Explain how you know.

yes ☐   no ☐

> Work out the number of boys and girls who pick their nose, remembering that more boys than girls were asked.

....

.... **2 marks**

Line graphs

1. This graph show the temperature change in a desert from afternoon to night.

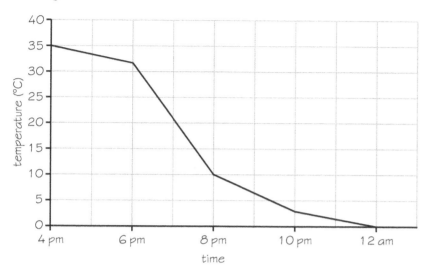

To find the temperature at a certain time, read up from the time axis and across to the temperature axis.

a) What is the approximate temperature at 9 pm? ....

b) Between which two times does the temperature

   drop most quickly? ....

The steeper the line, the faster the change.

c) What is the difference in temperature between

   4 pm and 8 pm? ....

d) At approximately what time is the temperature 5 °C? ....   **1 mark**

2. This graph shows the cost of sending a text message home from a different country at different times of day.

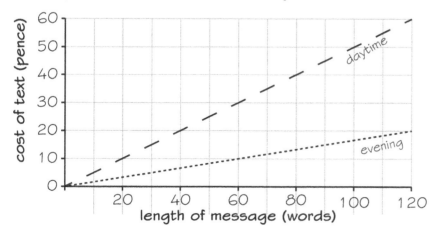

You will need to find the difference between the two values on the y-axis.

a) How much does it cost to send a 90-word message

   in the daytime? ....

b) How much more does it cost to send a 60-word message

   in the daytime than the evening? ....   **2 marks**

Drawing line graphs

1. This graph show the mean maximum temperatures in London throughout the year.

month	J	F	M	A	M	J	J	A	S	O	N	D
°C	9		12				23	23		16		10

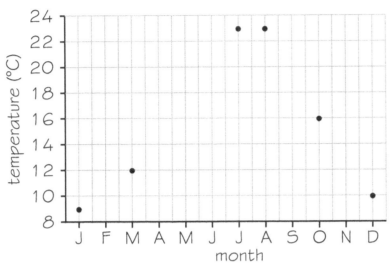

The table and the graph are incomplete. Here are the missing months and temperatures:

November 12°C, April 15°C, February 10°C, June 21°C, September 20°C, May 18°C.

a) Complete the table using the data above.

b) Plot the missing points on the graph.

c) Join the points with straight lines.

d) In which months is the temperature the same?

....

e) For how many months is the temperature over 14°C?

....

> Go across from the vertical scale and up from the horizontal scale.

> Try placing a ruler horizontally across the graph at 14°C to help you see the relevant points.

5 marks

Mean average

1. Find the mean of the values in each set.

   a) 10, 2, 18, 6, 4 ....

   b) 52, 13, 34 ....

   c) 1.5, 11, 8.5, 0.5, 1.5, 1 ....

   d) 1, 3, 2, 4 ....

   > Add all the values and then divide the total by the number of values.

   4 marks

2. Dillon wears a fitness tracker. Here are his daily steps for the week.

This week	
Monday	10,000
Tuesday	15,000
Wednesday	21,000
Thursday	9,000
Friday	4,000
Saturday	10,000
Sunday	8,000

   What is the mean number of steps he takes each day?

   ....

   ....

   .... **2 marks**

3. Draw an arrow that points to the mean of the numbers shown on each number line below.

   a)

   2 3 4 5 6 7 8 9 10 11 12 13 14 15

   b)

   9 10 11 12 13 14 15 16 17 18 19

   c)

   −10 −9 −8 −7 −6 −5 −4 −3 −2 −1 0 1 2 3 4 5 6 7 8 9 10

   3 marks

Mean problems

1. The heights of a group of four children are shown in this table. Their mean height is 128 cm. One of the values is missing.

children	height
Chad	120 cm
Dennis	132 cm
Anwyn	.........cm
Theresa	124 cm
mean:	128 cm

> The total height of all the children is 4 × 128 cm. Use subtraction to find the missing value.

How tall is Anwyn?

....   **2 marks**

2. Here is a bar chart showing the average hours of daily sunshine over one summer.

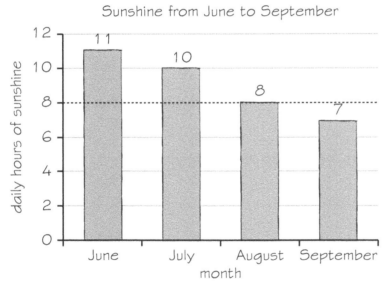

Sunshine from June to September

Brodie has drawn a dotted line on the bar chart. He says the line shows the mean number of hours of sunshine over the whole summer.

a) You don't agree with where Brodie has drawn the line. Explain why he is wrong.

....

....

....   **2 marks**

> You must use the values from the chart and calculations to prove your answer.

b) Draw a straight line to show accurately where the mean actually is.

1 mark

Answers

NUMBER

1 Place value

1.

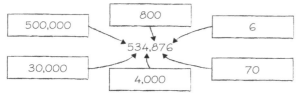

2. a) 2,643   b) 975,648   c) 6,614,215

3. a) Seven thousand, three hundred and ninety

   b) Eighteen thousand, three hundred and twenty-six

   c) Four hundred and fifty-five thousand, two hundred and one

2 Negative numbers

1. a) 9 degrees   b) 4 degrees
   c) 36 degrees   d) 30 degrees

2. a) −16, 2   b) −9, −6   c) −6, 4

3. 48.1 metres   4. 6 °C

3 Decimal numbers

1. a) 6.7   b) 9.43
   c) 18.528   d) 6.043

2.

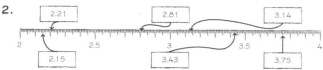

3. a) 4.6 > 4.06   b) 9.7 < 9.89
   c) 6.56 > 5.98   d) 23.5 > 2.35
   e) 2.22 < 2.222   f) 1.001 > 0.101

4. First Lucy (13.2 seconds), second Max (13.7 seconds), third Anil (14.7 seconds)

5. 7.456, 7.465, 7.564, 7.546, 7.645, 7.654

4 Rounding

1. a) 5,300   b) 8,400   c) 13,700

2. a) 4,000   b) 19,000   c) 548,000

3. a) 4,638,420 (to the nearest 10,000) is 4,640,000

   b) 4,637,300 (to the nearest 1,000,000) is 5,000,000

   c) 5,248,612 (to the nearest 1,000) is 5,249,000

   d) 5,220,230 (to the nearest 100,000) is 5,200,000

4. a) 7,452,540

To the nearest 1,000,000	7,000,000
To the nearest 100,000	7,500,000
To the nearest 10,000	7,450,000
To the nearest 1,000	7,453,000

   b) 4,250,500

To the nearest 1,000,000	4,000,000
To the nearest 100,000	4,300,000
To the nearest 10,000	4,250,000
To the nearest 1,000	4,251,000

5 Rounding decimals

1. a) 6.4   b) 4.7
   c) 13.9   d) 2.1

2. a) 8.66   b) 7.55
   c) 75.56   d) 27.08

3. 4.53   4.48   4.45

4. 6.98

5. a) 114.46   b) 3.14   c) 8.33
   d) 11.67   e) 3.38

6 Roman numerals

1.

2. a) 2,215   b) 1,550
   c) 1,945   d) 2,016

3. a) X + VI = XVI   b) MCDL − CCXXVII = MCCXXIII

4. Half past six (allow 6:30 or 18:30)

5. 7:20 or 19:20   6. 1984

7 Number and rounding problems

1. Any pair of **different** numbers that add together to make the given number, such as:

   a) X and VII + III   b) L and XXXVII + XIII
   c) M and DCC + CCC

2. a) 14.67 seconds

   b) 59.35 seconds   c) silver: Corinne gold: Nellie bronze: Niraj

3. a) Lower   b) Lower
   c) Higher   d) Lower

CALCULATION

8 Written addition

1. a) 9,948   b) 8,843
   c) 19,271   d) 551.77

2. £291.50

3. Bevan = 6,949 steps   Reuben = 7,189 steps

9 Written subtraction

1. a) 411   b) 315
   c) 312.2   d) 14,222
   e) 689   f) 136.88

2. 855 calories   3. £18.25

4. Amina's time = 12.65 seconds, Casey's time = 10.1 seconds

10 Estimating

1. a) 12,900 or 13,000   b) 1.5
   c) 5,000,000   d) £6

2. a) £73   b) £87

3. 4 hours   4. 40 metres

Answers

11 Add/subtract problems

1. 12 people   2. 24.4 miles   3. £1

12 Multiples

1. a) 76   24   8   b) 490   63
   c) 180   27   99   18   72   d) 366   354

2.

	multiple of 7	not a multiple of 7
even number	14 56	16 26 32
odd number	21 35 49	15 29

3. Any number that fits the criterion; most probable examples are given below.
   a) 12   24   36   48   60
   b) 24   48   72   96
   c) 9   18   27   36   45   54
   d) 35   70   105   140

4. 15

5. Yes, because any number ending in a 0 is even (so is a multiple of 2) and can be divided by 5 (so is a multiple of 5).

13 Factors

1. a) 1   2   3   6   7   14   21   42
   b) 1   3   5   15
   c) 1   2   3   4   6   8   9   12   18   24   36   72
   d) 1   13

2.

factors of 42	factors of 48
1	1
2	2
3	3
6	4
7	6
14	8
21	12
42	16
	24
	48

One mark for not including 19 or 25

One mark for putting 1, 2, 3 and 6 in both columns

One mark for all other correctly identified factors of 42

One mark for all other correctly identified factors of 48

3. 1 × 56   2 × 28   4 × 14   7 × 8

4. a) false   b) true   c) false

5. Yes, because 6 × 1,407 = 8,442 and 7 × 1,206 = 8,442.

14 Prime numbers

1. a) 2   3   5   7   b) 11   13   17   19
   c) 23   29   d) 31   37

2. a) False. 2 is an even prime number.
   b) True. Any number ending in 5 is divisible by 5.
   c) True. Its only factors are 1 and 109.

3. (Numbers can be in any order)
   a) 2 × 2 × 3   b) 2 × 2 × 2 × 7
   c) 5 × 5   d) 2 × 2 × 2 × 3 × 3

15 Square numbers

1.
   a) 6 × 6 = 6^2 = 36   b) 10 × 10 = 10^2 = 100
   c) 7 × 7 = 7^2 = 49   d) 11 × 11 = 11^2 = 121
   e) 3 × 3 = 3^2 = 9

2. a) 64   25   121   9   b) 16   4
   c) 81   144   36

3.

4. 36

5. 121

16 Cube numbers

1. a) 6 × 6 × 6 = 6^3 = 216
   b) 10 × 10 × 10 = 10^3 = 1,000
   c) 7 × 7 × 7 = 7^3 = 343
   d) 11 × 11 × 11 = 11^3 = 1,331
   e) 3 × 3 × 3 = 3^3 = 27

2. a) 64   27   125   b) 8   216
   c) 729   343

3.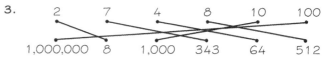

4. 216 tins of beans

5. Station Road = 343 cars   Church Street = 729 cars   Difference = 386 cars

17 Short multiplication

1. a) 2,180   b) 7,515
   c) 3,479   d) 12,750

2. a) 6   b) 1, 7   c) 8, 5   d) 5

3. 8,268 miles

18 Long multiplication

1. a) 1,104   b) 8,160
   c) 65,436   d) 745,998

2. a) £237,328   b) £19,162   c) £253,946

3. 83,016 miles.

19 Short division

1. a) 1,311   b) 903   c) 510   d) 1,824

2. a) >   b) <   c) >   d) >

3. £950

4. 715 metres

20 Long division

1. a) 14   b) 13
   c) $18\frac{1}{2}$ or 18.5   d) 118

2. 412 boxes   3. 263 miles

4. 123 cm

21 Order of operations

1. a) 44   b) 160   c) 5
   d) 5   e) 3   f) 120

2. a) $4 \times (3 + 2) = 20$

   b) $(6 + 3) \times 2 - 14 \div 2 = 11$

   c) $(5 + 5) \times 3 - 10 = 20$

   d) $6 \times (7 + 3) \div 2 + 1 = 31$

   e) $(2 + 3) \times (7 - 5) = 25$

3. $(\£47 - \£15) \div 2 + \£38 = \£54$

22 Solving problems

1. a) 95p   b) £3.70   c) 50p   d) £4.95

2. 251 packets of pasta   3. 113

4. Drinks = £2.55   Hot dogs = £3.75

23 Answering the question

1. 5 packets of cakes   2. 113 crates

3. £1,400

4. Pack of 6 (60p per bottle vs 65p per bottle).

FRACTIONS, DECIMALS AND PERCENTAGES

24 Fractions

1. a) Shaded: $\frac{3}{8}$ and unshaded: $\frac{5}{8}$

   b) Shaded: $\frac{4}{8} = \frac{1}{2}$ and unshaded: $\frac{4}{8} = \frac{1}{2}$

   c) Shaded: $\frac{2}{5}$ and unshaded: $\frac{3}{5}$

   d) Shaded: $\frac{4}{10} = \frac{2}{5}$ and unshaded: $\frac{6}{10} = \frac{3}{5}$

2. The answers are the same / represent the same fraction of the shape / they are equivalent.

3.

 a) $= \frac{3}{5}$ b) 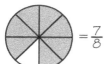 $= \frac{7}{8}$

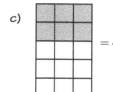 c) $= \frac{1}{3}$

4. $\frac{12}{36} = \frac{1}{3}$

25 Equivalent fractions

1. a) $\frac{4}{12}$ and $\frac{1}{3}$ b) $\frac{4}{20}$ and $\frac{1}{5}$ c) $\frac{5}{25}$ and $\frac{1}{5}$

2. a) $\frac{1}{4}$ b) $\frac{10}{35}$ and $\frac{21}{35}$

   c) $\frac{8}{12}$ and $\frac{9}{12}$ d) $\frac{5}{30}$ and $\frac{12}{30}$

3. a) $\frac{1}{4}$ b) $\frac{3}{8}$

   c) $\frac{7}{9}$ d) $\frac{8}{9}$

4. $\frac{16}{80} = \frac{1}{5}$ completed and $\frac{4}{5}$ left to do.

26 Fractions greater than l

1. a) $\frac{53}{8}$ b) $\frac{42}{15}$ c) $\frac{38}{3}$

   d) $\frac{1003}{10}$ e) $\frac{60}{14}$ f) $\frac{2210}{100}$

2. a) $1\frac{7}{8}$ b) $1\frac{1}{12}$ c) $50\frac{1}{2}$

   d) $2\frac{5}{27}$ e) $3\frac{1}{15}$ f) $1\frac{1}{2}$

3. 19

27 Comparing fractions

1. a) $\frac{6}{8} > \frac{38}{76}$ b) $\frac{253}{1000} > \frac{25}{100}$ c) $\frac{14}{4} > \frac{9}{3}$

2. $\frac{3}{8}$ $\frac{5}{12}$ $\frac{12}{24}$ $\frac{2}{3}$ $\frac{3}{4}$ $\frac{5}{6}$

3. Padma has written more.

4. Ruby has more chocolate left.

28 Add/subtract fractions

1. a) $\frac{7}{12}$ b) $\frac{29}{35}$

   c) $5\frac{7}{18}$ d) $11\frac{1}{2}$

2. a) $\frac{5}{7}$ b) $\frac{6}{35}$

   c) $1\frac{13}{18}$ d) $1\frac{1}{2}$

3. $1\frac{4}{9}$ metres

4. Luca's bags = $10\frac{3}{10}$ kg

   Cameron's bags = $9\frac{8}{10}$ kg

   Difference = $\frac{1}{2}$ kg

   Luca is carrying more. His bags are $\frac{1}{2}$ kg heavier.

29 Multiplying fractions

1.

Fraction	$\times \frac{1}{2}$	$\times \frac{1}{4}$	$\times \frac{1}{8}$
$\frac{1}{3}$	$\frac{1}{6}$	$\frac{1}{12}$	$\frac{1}{24}$
$\frac{1}{5}$	$\frac{1}{10}$	$\frac{1}{20}$	$\frac{1}{40}$
$\frac{1}{6}$	$\frac{1}{12}$	$\frac{1}{24}$	$\frac{1}{48}$
$\frac{1}{7}$	$\frac{1}{14}$	$\frac{1}{28}$	$\frac{1}{56}$

2. a) $\frac{1}{36}$ b) $\frac{6}{35}$ c) $\frac{3}{12}$ or $\frac{1}{4}$

   d) $\frac{1}{12}$ e) $\frac{1}{4}$ f) 25

3. Accept any correct pair, though most common include:

   a) $\frac{1}{2} \times \frac{1}{2}$ b) $\frac{1}{5} \times \frac{1}{5}$

   c) $\frac{1}{2} \times \frac{1}{4}$ d) $\frac{1}{3} \times \frac{2}{3}$

30 Dividing fractions

1.

fraction	$\div 2$	$\div 3$	$\div 4$
$\frac{1}{3}$	$\frac{1}{6}$	$\frac{1}{9}$	$\frac{1}{12}$
$\frac{1}{5}$	$\frac{1}{10}$	$\frac{1}{15}$	$\frac{1}{20}$
$\frac{1}{6}$	$\frac{1}{12}$	$\frac{1}{18}$	$\frac{1}{24}$
$\frac{1}{7}$	$\frac{1}{14}$	$\frac{1}{21}$	$\frac{1}{28}$

Answers

2. a) $\frac{1}{24}$ b) $\frac{1}{60}$ c) $\frac{1}{6}$

3.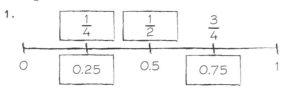

$\frac{1}{2} \div 3$ $\frac{1}{6} \div 3$ $\frac{1}{5} \div 3$ $\frac{1}{4} \div 3$

$\frac{1}{3} \div 6$ $\frac{1}{3} \div 4$ $\frac{1}{3} \div 2$ $\frac{1}{3} \div 5$

4. Table 1 = $\frac{1}{8}$ Table 2 = $\frac{1}{12}$

31 Equivalent decimals and fractions

1.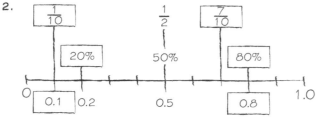

2. a) $\frac{1}{2}$ or 0.5 b) $\frac{1}{4}$ or 0.25 c) $\frac{1}{5}$ or 0.2

3. a) 0.25 b) 0.5
   c) 0.2 d) 0.125

4. a) $\frac{5}{10}$ b) $\frac{10}{40}$
   c) $\frac{5}{25}$ d) $\frac{75}{100}$

32 Multiplying decimals

1. a) 6.5   65   650
   b) 92.5   925   9,250

2. a) 1.05 b) 49.76
   c) 24.57 d) 40.1

3. 1.36 × 3 = 4.08 litres   4. £19.12

33 Percentages

1. a) 56% b) 44%

2.

3. 50%
4. 20%

34 Converting percentages

1. a) $\frac{1}{5}$ b) $\frac{3}{20}$ c) $\frac{3}{4}$
   d) $\frac{21}{25}$ e) $\frac{33}{50}$ f) $\frac{1}{20}$

2. a) 25% b) 40% c) 80%
   d) 44% e) 68% f) 40%

3. 40%
4. 55%

35 Percentages of amounts

1. a) 12 b) $47\frac{1}{2}$ c) 40
   d) 150 e) 32 f) 36

2. a) 36 b) 99 c) 42
3. 65%
4. a) 150 children b) 75 children c) 25 children

36 Solving percentage problems

1. a) 50 b) 30 c) 35 d) 25
2. 4 pieces of cake are left.
3. a) 20% of £120 b) 80% of £200
   c) 70% of £10 d) 5% of £100,000
4. Ava

RATIO AND PROPORTION

37 Ratio

1. 3 : 2 and 7 : 3
2. Note any arrangement is acceptable provided the correct number of boxes have been coloured.
   a) 1 grey : 5 white

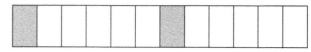

   b) 4 grey : 2 white

3. 4 : 1
4. 7 : 5
5. 2 : 3

38 Proportion

1. a) $\frac{1}{4}$ b) $\frac{1}{4}$ c) $\frac{1}{2}$
2. a) $\frac{1}{3}$ b) $\frac{2}{3}$
3. a) $\frac{4}{9}$ b) $\frac{5}{9}$
4. a) $\frac{1}{10}$ b) $\frac{3}{10}$ c) $\frac{6}{10} = \frac{3}{5}$

39 Scale factors

1. A = 4 cm   B = 6 cm   C = 6 cm
2. Scale factor = 7

3.

scale factor	A	B	C
2	4 cm	6 cm	8 cm
5	10 cm	15 cm	20 cm
10	20 cm	30 cm	40 cm
$\frac{1}{2}$	1 cm	1.5 cm	2 cm

4. $1\frac{1}{2}$ × 10 cm = 15 cm

40 Unequal sharing and grouping

1. One group should have 14 buttons and the other should have 21
2. There are 20 yellow and 5 red cubes
3. One person gets £60 and the other person gets £100
4. There are 10 boys in the class

41 Ratio problems

1.

butter (g)	sugar (g)	milk (ml)
100	450	150
200	900	300
1,000	4,500	1,500
50	225	75

2. a) 100 ml   b) 2 full bottles

3. One person gets £1,920 and one person gets £2,880.

ALGEBRA

42 Using letters

1. a) $d = 100$ b) $f = 11$
   c) $h = 63$ d) $b = 28$

2. $m \times 4 = 24$, $24 \div 4 = 6$, $m = 6$

3. $a = 9$, $b = 9$, $c = 9$, $d = 4$, code = 9994

4. $h + 12 - 9 = 50$, $h + 12 = 50 + 9$, $h + 12 = 59$, $h = 59 - 12$, $h = 47$

43 Simple formulae

1. £20

2. £28.50

3. 4 games with no instructions would cost £16. There would be £0.75 left. $3 \times £0.25 = £0.75$ so he buys 3 sets of instructions.

4. She buys 2 video games.

44 Linear sequences

1. 3, 10, 17, 24, 31, 38, 45, 52, 59

2. a) 38, 33, 28, 23, 18, 13, 8, 3
   b) First term = 38, subtract 5 from the previous term

3. 7, 11, 15, 19, 23, 27, 31, 35, 39

4. 19, 25, 31, 37, 43, 49

5. 5

45 Two unknowns

1. There are several possible answers. Answers might include:

   white = 1   black = 5
   white = 2   black = 6
   white = 3   black = 7

2.

$p + 6 = q$	$q - 3 = p$	$p - 5 = q$	$q + 7 = p$
2, 8; 1, 7	8, 5; 7, 4; 6, 3; 5, 2; 4, 1	8, 3; 7, 2; 6, 1	1, 8

3. No. If m is 4, then $4 + 7 - 2 = 9$, which means n must be 9 not 8.

46 Combination problems

1.

black boots	black sandals	black trainers	black wellies
brown boots	brown sandals	brown trainers	brown wellies
green boots	green sandals	green trainers	green wellies

2.

tea and milk	tea and sugar	tea and cream
coffee and milk	coffee and sugar	coffee and cream
hot chocolate and milk	hot chocolate and sugar	hot chocolate and cream

3. Scores could have been: 0–0, 1–0, 0–1, 1–1, 2–0, 0–2, 2–1, 1–2, 2–2

4. Answers may vary. **10** farmers (20 legs) + **20** sheep (80 legs); **20** farmers (40 legs) + **15** sheep (60 legs); **30** farmers (60 legs) + **10** sheep (40 legs)

47 Algebra problems

1. Circle = 2p, Diamond = 20p

2. $h = 7.5$ cm, $l = 15$ cm

3. $b = 3$ cm

MEASUREMENT

48 Reading scales

1. False, true, true

2. Jug A contains 400 ml and jug B contains 325 ml so jug B contains less juice.

49 Converting units

1. Incorrect, 7.2 m = 720 cm; Correct; Incorrect, 1160 g = 1.160 kg; Correct

2. a) 1500 g   b) 270 ml

3. Total wingspan = 145 mm

50 Ordering measures

1.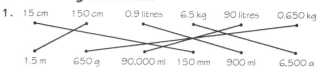

   15 cm   150 cm   0.9 litres   6.5 kg   90 litres   0.650 kg

   1.5 m   650 g   90,000 ml   150 mm   900 ml   6.500 g

2. a) true   b) false   c) true

3. a) <   b) <   c) >
   d) >   e) <   f) >

4. a) 2,100 cm, 2 km, 2,050 m, 2,500 m
   b) 1,025 ml, 1250 ml, 1.255 l, 1,350 ml
   c) 10 g, 0.1 kg, 1,500 g, 15,000 g

51 Imperial units

1. 3 litres

2. a) 10 stone   b) 60 kg

3. a) 16 km   b) 160 km

52 Measure calculations

1. a) 0.56 kg   b) 98 cm   c) 1,770 ml
   d) 4.5 cm   e) 630 g   f) 9.2 m

2. a) 780 g   b) 160 cm
   c) 6.25 m   d) 700 ml

53 Time

1. a) 2 minutes 10 seconds   b) 210 minutes
   c) 2 years and 5 weeks   d) 2 centuries

2. a) 10:30   b) 20:45   c) 00:25

3. a) 75 minutes   b) 125 minutes

54 Perimeter and area

1. a) 30 cm², 22 cm   b) 48 cm², 32 cm
   c) 63 m², 48 m   d) 25 mm², 25 mm

2. 24 cm

3. 72 cm

Answers

55 Compound shapes

1. 50 cm
2. 62 cm
3. 320 cm or 3.2 m

56 Areas of triangles

1. **a)** 6 cm²   **b)** 6 cm²
2. Yes. The area of the junior playground is 300 m² and the area of the infant playground is 250 m², making a total of 550 m².

57 Areas of parallelograms

1. **a)** 90 cm²   **b)** 210 cm²
2. Answers may vary: any parallelogram with an area of 15 cm².
3. 120 cm²

58 Volumes of cuboids

1. **a)** 36 m³   **b)** 9,000 mm³   **c)** 125 cm³
2. **a)** 24 more cubes
   b) Multiple answers: any 3 numbers that make 30 when multiplied together i.e. 2, 3 and 5

GEOMETRY

59 2D shape properties

1. **a)** equilateral triangle   **b)** regular octagon
2. **a)** D   **b)** C, D   **c)** A, C, D
3. Answers may vary. For example:

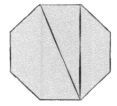

60 Naming 2D shapes

1. top left: rectangle   top right: trapezium
   bottom left: kite   bottom right: parallelogram
2. top left: equilateral, 3 equal sides, 3 equal angles
   top right: isosceles, 2 equal sides, 2 equal angles
   bottom left: scalene, 0 equal sides, 0 equal angles
   bottom right: equilateral, 3 equal sides, 3 equal angles
3. top left: regular   top right: irregular
   bottom left: irregular   bottom right: regular

61 Naming 3D shapes

1. top left: cube, prism   top right: tetrahedron, trapezium
   bottom left: sphere, curved faces
   bottom right: pentagonal prism, prism
2. 8 faces, 12 vertices, 18 edges
3.

shape	faces	vertices	edges
cuboid	6	8	12
square pyramid	5	5	8
cylinder	3	0	2

62 Nets

1. From left to right: cube, octahedron, tetrahedron, triangular prism

2.

3.

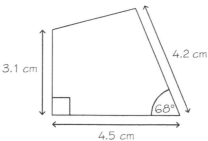

63 Angles

1. **a)** acute   **b)** reflex
   c) obtuse   **d)** reflex
2. **a)** obtuse   **b)** reflex
   c) obtuse   **d)** acute
3. $x = 20°$ (acute); $y = 100°$ (obtuse); $z = 30°$ (acute)

64 Calculating angles

1. **a)** 30° + 100° + 50° = 180°
   b) 180° + 100° + 80° = 360°
   c) 15° + 45° + 120° = 180°
   d) 200° + 90° + 25° + 45° = 360°
2. (from left to right) top row: 140°, 70°, 150°, bottom row: 150°, 45°, 45°
3. 140°

65 Drawing 2D shapes

1. Triangle drawn with lengths 10 cm, 6 cm, 8 cm
2. Quadrilateral with lengths 3.1 cm, 4.5 cm and 4.2 cm labelled and accurately drawn.

3.1 cm   4.2 cm   68°   4.5 cm

3. $y = 106°$ (allow 105° to 107°)

66 Circles

1. **a)** radius   **b)** circumference   **c)** diameter
2. 5.8 cm → diameter   18.2 cm → circumference
   2.9 cm → radius
3. 4.5 cm

67 Coordinates

1. A is at (3, 8); B is at (2, 2) ; C is at (9, 2)
2. (3, 3)
3. (−1, −2)

68 Translations

1. a)

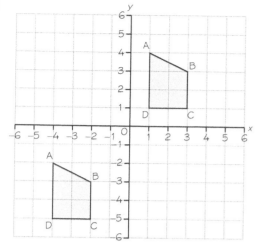

b) B(−2, −3), C(−2, −5), D(−4, −5)

c) A(0, 0), B(2, −1), C(2, −3), D(0, −3)

69 Reflection

1.

2. a)

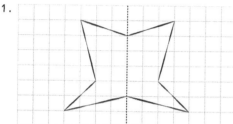

b) M(4, −1), N(2, −1)

STATISTICS

70 Tables

1. a) frequencies: a–e = 7, f–j = 6, k–o = 8, p–t = 7, u–z = 7

b) k–o   c) a–e, p–t and u–z   d) 13

2. a) 32 minutes   b) 11:09

c) 11:37   d) 11:29

71 Bar charts

1. a) 8   b) 7

c) Yes, because the girls swam a total of 31 lengths but the boys swam a total of 38, a difference of 7.

2. a) Vertical axis labelled in intervals of 2; horizontal axis labelled comedy, adventure, autobiography, horror

b) Horror bar drawn exactly 5 units high (measured on vertical axis)

72 Pie charts

1. a) $\frac{1}{2}$ b) 21

2. a) 9   b) 8

c) No. 21 boys pick their nose but only 6 girls do.

73 Line graphs

1. a) 7 °C   b) 6–8pm

c) 25 degrees   d) 9:30pm

2. a) 45p   b) 20p

74 Drawing line graphs

1. a)

month	J	F	M	A	M	J	J	A	S	O	N	D
°C	9	10	12	15	18	21	23	23	20	16	12	10

b), c)

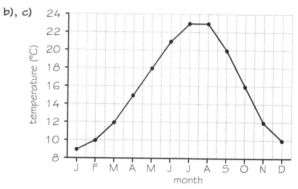

d) July and August, February and December, March and November

e) 7 months (April to October)

75 Mean average

1. a) 8   b) 33

c) 4   d) 2.5

2. 11,000 steps

3. a) arrow points to 6   b) arrow points to $15\frac{1}{3}$

c) arrow points to −1

76 Mean problems

1. 136 cm

2. a) The mean is 9 because 11 + 10 + 8 + 7 = 36 and 36 ÷ 4 = 9

b)

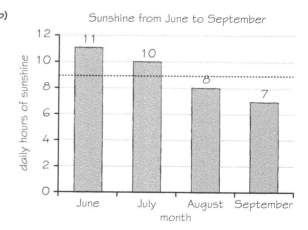

Sunshine from June to September

Published by Pearson Education Limited, 80 Strand, London, WC2R 0RL.

www.pearsonschools.co.uk

Text © Pearson Education Limited 2016
Edited by Saskia Besier
Typeset by Jouve India Private Limited
Produced by Elektra Media
Original illustrations © Pearson Education Limited 2016
Illustrated by Elektra Media
Cover illustration by Ana Albero

The rights of Giles Clare and Paul Flack to be identified as authors of this work have been asserted by them in accordance with the Copyright, Designs and Patents Act 1988.

First published 2016

British Library Cataloguing in Publication Data
A catalogue record for this book is available from the British Library.

ISBN 978 1 292 14628 7